THE MINORITY CAREER BOOK

THE
MINORITY
CAREER
BOOK

Miquela Rivera, Ph. D.

BOB ADAMS, INC.
P U B I S H E R S

Published by Bob Adams, Inc.
260 Center Street, Holbrook, MA 02343

Hardcover ISBN: 1-55850-013-8
Paperback ISBN: 1-55850-012-X

Printed in the United States of America

B   C   D   E   F   G   H   I   J

This publication is designed to provide accurate and authoritative information with regard to the subject matter covered. It is sold with the understanding that the publisher is not engaged in rendering legal, accounting, or other professional advice. If legal advice or other expert assistance is required, the services of a qualified professional person should be sought.
— From a *Declaration of Principles* jointly adopted by a Committee of the American Bar Association and a Committee of Publishers and Associations.

Author's Note

Many of the chapters or sections of chapters in this book were originally in the *Hispanic Engineer* and *US Black Engineer* magazines and the *Tucson Citizen* newspaper. Credit goes to career Communications of Baltimore, Maryland, and the *Tucson Citizen*, published by Gannett Co., for permission to revise these works for this book.

Dedication

To Mom and Dad, with love and gratitude.

Acknowledgments

Many thanks to: Ray and Carmela Mellado, for seeing my potential, encouraging it, and providing many opportunities across the years; Judi Schuler, for guidance and assistance in preparing this book; my loving family, who has provided encouragement and support across the years; and my husband, Marvin Lozano, for his insight, patience, and love.

Contents

Part I

Get Ready

Chapter 1

To Reach the
Winner's Circle

Minority professionals on their way to the top need one major ingredient to succeed—they need to be prepared. This book can assist you in your preparation by helping you understand the challenges you face and the options you have entering today's work world. It may also help coworkers and supervisors identify and better understand the particular experiences and different viewpoints each minority professional brings to the work place.

Equally important, this book can help everyone realize that minority professionals bring unique talents and valuable assets to their professions and that these professionals have what it takes to be successful.

To reach the winner's circle, you need to be prepared, focus your direction, and stick with your plans. A prepared course of action can help you accomplish these goals.

This first section of this book, "Get Ready," focuses on the importance of goal setting and technical preparation for minority professionals. A strong sense of mission, a clear focus, and a solid education make all the difference. What you know matters, and so does how you use your knowledge.

The second section, "Get Set," focuses on the expectations, beliefs, values, and attitudes minorities bring to their work. Cultural diversity, discipline, seeking opportunities, paying the price, and ethics are discussed from a minority professional's point of view. The ways minority professionals think are crucial to success. Look within yourself to aim in the right direction.

Prepared and focused, you must then know how to survive. The third section of the book, "Go!" focuses on techniques for surviving and excelling in the work place. Office politics, being the "only" one in a job, gaining legitimacy and recognition, taking risks, dealing with others, taking care of yourself, developing leadership skills, enjoying your rewards, and preparing for continual change are some of the topics discussed.

This book isn't a cure-all for every problem you may experience as a minority professional in the work place. It doesn't contain foolproof approaches or all the "right" answers. But it does look carefully at issues minority professionals face at home and on the job. It offers positive alternatives, useful techniques, and a conceptual framework for understanding "being different." Equally important, it offers suggestions for allowing yourself to enjoy success while keeping your eye on the goals ahead.

Chapter 2

Creating a Vision

Ask any winner the secret to success and he or she will probably reply, "Decide what you want to do, then do it!" It may seem simple, but it's not always easy. What you choose to do with your life, why you make the choices you make, and how you relate to success are crucial to getting ahead.

When you think of success or prosperity, what images come to mind? Perhaps you envision a BMW, summer vacations in Europe, or a "getaway" beach house. People usually think of success or prosperity mainly in economic terms. Money has a bearing on what you can do, but money alone is *not* prosperity.

Prosperity really means having a life of choice. Successful living is doing what you want to do, not simply what you have to do. For a successful, prosperous person, life doesn't just happen; it's celebrated. For the successful minority professional, it means having options family or friends may not have, having the freedom to excel—not merely survive—

and being able to meet the challenges of making a positive difference for others, regardless of your field of interest.

As a minority professional, prosperity is important to you, even if you haven't thought much about it. You should be concerned about it because you have a chance to make a difference, and it would be a shame if you missed your chance. The first part of the chapter focuses on ten principles that can guide you on the path to success.

Principle 1

Thinking makes success and prosperity a reality.

There's a fine line between the ideal in your mind and what can become reality in your life. Your mind is capable of creating the kind of life you've always wanted, but you must be willing to develop your creative ideas and act on them so that events in your life flow smoothly and abundantly.

Principle 2

It's important to know what you want and why you want it.

Success and prosperity are a state of mind in which you live life as you wish. It's crucial for you to know your priorities, your passions, your sense of mission, and your drive. For most professionals, the issue is not survival but determining what to do with their lives. It's the search for ways to make a difference in this world and the need for living a life that matters.

If you choose a goal exclusively to earn money, achieve fame, gain status, or for any reason other than making a difference for others, you may lower your chances for success. Even if you do "make it" financially, self-centered goals seldom give long-lasting satisfaction, true success, and a deep sense of prosperity.

Principle 3

Planning results in consistent success and prosperity.

Most people spend more time planning their vacation than they do planning their careers. They put tremendous energy into planning a wedding, but they fail to plan their marriage. They'll hunt for a bargain but ignore the long-range financial picture.

If you don't know where you're going, anywhere will do. If you don't have a plan, you might just end up there. To clarify the course of your life, try the following.

1. Write down what you would like to achieve in six months, a year, five years, ten years, and twenty years. Be specific. Don't worry that things are too small or too great. Note them anyway. After five years your goals probably become more vague or repetitious. Most people tend to overestimate what they can do in a year and underestimate what they can do in ten.

2. Write down what you would do if you won the lottery and had all the money you needed.

3. Pretend you have one day to live. Money is no problem, so you can do whatever you want. Write down what important things you'd want to do.

4. In one sentence, write your life's purpose. Identify what kind of contribution you want to make to the world.

5. Write down how you would like to be remembered. An epitaph reading "World-Famous Millionaire" differs immensely from "Loving Father" or "Devoted Mother."

Look over your lists, and ask yourself whether you are already working toward some of your goals. Are you already doing some of the things you would do if you only had one day to live? Take note of the things you can do that don't require huge sums of money. Look at the bottom line and see what's most important to you. Focus clearly on the basics; they will guide your life's course.

When it comes to your career, apply the same principles. Identify what's most important to you and how you would like to make a difference. Capture the essence of what you want to do professionally, then set your sights for that.

You may you want to be a schoolteacher, but if the heart of what you want to do is to teach someone to read, you could also be a literacy volunteer. Or try being a parent! Capturing the essence of what you want to do is important because it focuses your goal while broadening the means by which you can achieve it.

Principle 4

Everything happens for your benefit.

The world has its own flow in which there is enough for all if we are open to it. This doesn't mean that everything will run smoothly or that you won't have any problems. Instead, it means you accept life as it comes and view problems as opportunities to grow. The prosperity principle takes you from expecting people or events to change to suit you, to understanding your role in events and learning and growing. With the philosophy of prosperity, you do not fail. Instead, you learn to switch directions.

The Philosophy of Scarcity states that life and its resources are limited. Nothing is enough. Money, sex, gadgets, fame, real estate—someone will always have more. If you're a scarcity thinker, you'll probably feel cheated.

Scarcity thinkers view things negatively or in terms of loss. Ventures or problems are win/lose situations; win/win situations seem almost inconceivable.

Pilots define attitude as the degree to which they can see above or below the horizon. Look at your point of view and ask yourself whether you're headed in the right direction. What are your assumptions about life and what it offers? Maybe you feel there's enough, or maybe you feel you must compete to get your share. Your ease, confidence, and ability to tolerate frustration largely depend on the philosophy you choose.

Principle 5

The more I see my role in and my contribution to every situation, the more easily I can maintain my energy and experience success.

Ask yourself whether you attribute your problems or setbacks to "bad luck" or whether you recognize your role in a given situation. If you recognize that you tend to give up easily when things get tough, you won't be as apt to blame the situation for being "against you." If you believe there are no good potential mates left in the world, chances are you're picking inappropriate ones and allowing them to remain in your life. If you know someone who complains constantly about a job he hates, he's probably not doing much to change his situation.

Principle 6

To experience success, you must match your goals and desires to your true self.

People sometimes sabotage their own success when they insist on following a goal that doesn't suit their personality, values, interests, physical abilities, or desires, or if they've decided on a goal strictly for selfish reasons, such as personal gain. Ask yourself whether your activities are congruent with what you want and whether you want something that will also be useful to others.

Being an accountant because Dad wanted you to be one, not because it's your heart's desire, guarantees you one thing: you'll be a miserable accountant and your clients will know it. Even if you're financially successful, if it isn't what you truly want to do, success will be hollow.

Principle 7

You attract people and situations similar to what you are.

If you don't want to spend time with turkeys, don't be one. When it comes to developing your career, you will attract people with similar goals if you have a sense of direction and drive.

If you find yourself in a situation in which things don't feel "right," chances are you're dealing with people who are unlike you.

You'll probably have to leave and find something more suitable. If you don't like the way your life is going, look in the mirror first. Once *you* change, other things will also change.

Principle 8

You've already got what it takes.

It's difficult to be successful or feel prosperous if you have a limited sense of self-acceptance. Waiting for those extra fifteen pounds to melt away before you buy that special outfit, holding off having friends over until you get a bigger house, waiting until the "time is right" or there is "enough money" to travel, have children, or do any of the things you want to do, blocks your ability to enjoy what life offers.

Accepting yourself as you are now removes that negative inner struggle. It also frees you to take positive steps toward your goals.

Principle 9

Maintain an attitude of forgiveness for your sake and the sake of others.

One of the most common road blocks to prosperity and success is the need to forgive. Grudges that have been carried for years take up the space and mental energy that goals and success would otherwise occupy.

Make a list of resentments you still hold from throughout your life. List who was involved and why you resented what happened. Then think about your role in events. Perhaps you needed to control the situation, or maybe the person threatened your emotional security. Maybe pride, lust, or greed got in the way.

Forgive yourself for not taking a more productive role in the situation, then forgive the other person for his or her wrongdoing. Learn what your options are, and move on. The sooner you release any grudge you hold against yourself or against another person, the sooner you'll feel negative energy evaporate and positive energy begin.

Principle 10

Get rid of "excess baggage" to make room for what you do want.

People often hesitate to let go of old behaviors, old relationships, or old possessions before they are assured of new ones. But you won't have room for new ones as long as the old ones are taking up space!

Whether it's making room in your closet for new clothes or freeing yourself of negative relationships to find appropriate ones, releasing yourself from the old ensures you'll receive new. If you're clear on how you want your life to be, that's what you'll probably receive—if you make room for it.

FOLLOW THE PATH TO SUCCESS

After becoming clear on what you want in life and why, the "how" will become apparent. If becoming educated is your goal, school or some other learning experience seems logical. The key to maintaining clarity is concentration. If there are too many distractions, too many goals, conflicting desires, or other things that tend to scatter your forces, it will be difficult to concentrate.

Simplify when you can. Think basic. Remind yourself of what you're doing and why and work toward it daily. Scattered attention produces fragmented results. Fine-tune your concentration, and success will follow.

Be Flexible

Things don't always work out as you planned, but that's no accident. It's no catastrophe, either. We often have an idea of how we want things to be. When they don't turn out exactly right, we might assume our desires were not met. Look again. What we want and how we want it often differ from what we get, but usually it's a matter of form.

Things come in alternative ways, so you must be alert and open to seeing them. If your goal is to help older people, working in a nursing home is not the only way to do it. Being a social worker, volunteering services in a center for the aged, or visiting the infirm all qualify as ways of meeting that goal.

You must be flexible enough to keep your eye on the goal instead of rigidly focusing on only one way to get things get done.

Speak Up for Yourself

Being timid doesn't help anyone; it's up to you to let people know what you need. It's also important to learn to protect yourself from people and situations that may be harmful to you. Maintaining a clear vision of what you're doing prevents others from taking advantage of you. To know what is best for yourself and to pursue it with honor and reason allows good things to flow to you in return.

Recheck Your Direction

Periodically recheck the direction you're taking in your life. Needs, desires, and circumstances change. Ask yourself whether you should change, drop, alter, or add to your goals. Rethinking the "whys" of what you are doing automatically realigns the "whats" and "hows." If you're sure of where you're going, it's only a matter of time before you get there.

Chapter 3

Technical Preparation Is Important

No matter what anyone tells you, education is important. A formal education can help you in many ways.

- □ It holds the key that will open the door, giving you opportunities that wouldn't be open to you any other way.

- □ It introduces you to a way of thinking, of solving problems, and of being creative that is different from intuitive or other informal thinking.

- □ It prepares you to stay with something long enough to succeed, despite the many obstacles you may face.

- It gives you the opportunity to accomplish something and enjoy it, even if it's simply for its own sake.

- It equips you with technical information crucial to advancement and success as a professional.

For minorities, formal education is essential for these reasons and more. If you're the first in your family to achieve academically, education will allow you to "break the mold" and enter into a new professional area and lifestyle. Education will demonstrate that it's not only who you know but *what* you know that matters.

A BALANCED CURRICULUM

With today's fast-track training in the field of high technology, it's easy for a student to load his or her education with large doses of science to the neglect of other subjects, such as humanities. By the same token, students who lean toward the arts need to balance out their education with science and mathematics.

Regardless of your particular interests, a balance in your formal education is essential if you are to survive and prosper as a professional in the future. Expertise solely in one area is not enough to survive in today's changing work world.

Americans often look to science and technology for answers. But human and technical problems require an understanding of how manmade solutions fit into the scheme of life itself. Today, people in technology need to blend information and compassion. Formal schooling helps build skills and increases know-how; compassion is enhanced through the liberal arts.

Liberal arts are crucial to the development and application of science and technology. The scientific method provides a systematic way of finding information; the humanities provide a framework to apply that information meaningfully. Developing a strain of corn to feed a starving nation will do little good if the people won't eat corn. Without knowledge of history, government, anthropology, and psychology, concrete scientific solutions are useless. A strong background in liberal arts helps the scientist place accurate information within a human context. It turns an answer into a viable solution.

People with social science or liberal arts backgrounds need equally to balance their knowledge with skills in mathematics and science. Such a balance prepares a person to deal effectively in the high-tech world of work. When the sensitivity and understanding gained through studying the humanities is coupled with technological learning, beauty and utility can result. Architects, for example, ideally design for function and aesthetics. Musicians work with rhythms and melodies, both based in mathematics, allied with personal expression and interpretation.

A balanced curriculum helps a person see how science is interlocked with many aspects of life. It places concrete facts in the realm of human experience. The human experience from a philosophical approach takes on a new, meaningful, predictable form when scientific knowledge is added.

Problem solving also takes on a different tone if a person has a well-rounded education. Technology in itself will not solve problems or save humanity from political or social disasters. Only people who are grounded in a full understanding of life can do so.

RESPONSIBILITIES OF MINORITY PROFESSIONALS

For minority professionals, competence in science *and* the humanities is crucial. Most professionals want to make a

29

relevant contribution in their field. To be a minority concerned about the advancement of your own group is important, but to be a minority skilled with technical answers and that sense of mission is powerful. Interdisciplinary balance in competence is the key to making a difference.

Look objectively at your professional training. If it's too heavily weighted in your technical-content area, perhaps you need to round out your education. If you're an engineer and find you have little background in literature or music, those disciplines might add a dimension to the way you view your work and deal with other people that engineering alone can't give. If you studied English, you may need to increase your knowledge of mathematics and science.

To succeed as a professional in a high-tech world, you need to keep up with scientific advancements. But to be a well-rounded citizen who seeks reasonable solutions and makes meaningful contributions, you need the balance a varied curriculum provides.

Going Back to School as a Professional

Employed professionals who already have a degree decide to go back to school for a variety of reasons. Sometimes it's a matter of economics. Advanced training opens opportunities for a better position with higher pay. For others, an advanced degree or professional training is a job requirement, with costs assumed by the employer. In this case, returning to school is the price you pay for job security.

Returning to school can be an effective way to address job burnout, limited job opportunities, or unemployment in a specific industry. Professionals who find themselves facing any of these conditions may seek additional education to help them move into another professional area. "I knew I couldn't face another day in the classroom," one former teacher told me. "I absolutely *had* to make a change."

Most often, professionals return to school to expand their technical skills and to keep up with the changing job market. Developments in science and technology occur so rapidly that even the most dedicated professional finds it difficult to keep abreast of changes. Going back to school is a more efficient way to catch up and move ahead.

Returning students often remark that going back is, "something I've always wanted to do." They are on the threshold of growing and changing because it's a natural thing for them to do.

Many decisions and adjustments must be made by a professional returning to school. The logistics of work hours, duties, and pay need to be addressed with employers. Sometimes families need to change their routines to accommodate new schedules. Household and personal budgets often need revamping to allow for the added expense (and possibly reduced earnings) of returning to school.

Prospective students need to answer specific questions about the courses they plan to take. Continuing in one field or switching to another, deciding whether a new field will prepare you for what you want to do professionally, selecting a school that is reasonable, available, and strong in the technical area you seek, and reviewing your own academic preparedness are crucial factors in returning to school.

Minorities are often steered into vocational trades as they leave high school. Welding, cosmetology, and auto repair are frequently named as fields minority high school students are "good at" pursuing. For minorities who desire to further their education and enter the professions, a similar dilemma exists. Ethnic minorities are often channeled into education, foreign languages, ethnic studies, and physical education. Women have traditionally gravitated toward the classroom or sickroom to build their careers.

A minority professional returning to school must refocus his or her goals and weigh the choices. If you've become known as the "minority professional" in your field, it may be more difficult to diversify. You must assess how hospitable a discipline or a school is to minorities. A lack of role models often makes a field seem closed to a minority person who is exploring it. If you decide to switch, your academic background must again be strong.

A professional returning to school must often work to support a family and pay tuition costs. A new field, an inadequate academic background, few role models, an inhospitable field of study and the need to work can dilute your scholarly efforts and make returning to school even more difficult.

> Emily, a thirty-six-year-old registered nurse, decided to pursue a doctorate in counseling after twelve years of working. "The scary part," she related, "began when I entered the classroom. Suddenly I wondered if I was too old to be there. Everyone else looked so young. They seemed so sharp that I wondered if I was smart enough to compete. I hadn't been in a classroom for a long time, and I was afraid I didn't know how to study and wouldn't be able to keep up with the work. I didn't know the professors or the politics in the department, either, and everyone else knew the ropes. They all seemed to be great friends, and I didn't know a soul."
>
> Emily went ahead anyway and oiled her study skills. She formed a few friendships and became acquainted with her professors. She learned to become an "efficient" student and make every minute count.
>
> "The hardest thing," Emily remembered, "was losing status. I'd been a nursing supervisor for a long time. Suddenly my work experience didn't seem to count for much compared to all the theory they were teaching. After awhile, I learned to apply that theory to my own experiences, even if I couldn't always share it with someone."
>
> After completing her doctorate, Emily reflected that she had learned a lot about counseling and research methods. "More than that," she added, "I've learned about working with other people and about the political struggles they get into. But mostly I've learned about myself. I actually did it!"

Although continuing school has its benefits, more people don't return for reasons discussed below.

BARRIERS TO RETURNING TO SCHOOL

Money and time are the two barriers most often cited by professionals who decided they could not return to school. They either had time but no money or money but no time. Sometimes they didn't have money *or* time!

Stretching money and time requires a great many personal sacrifices on the part of the returning student and his or her loved ones. These sacrifices begin with discipline, and discipline requires a lot of effort and energy. In a world filled with messages to "live for the moment," the joys of learning can seem remote, especially if you're weary or discouraged. In an era of high technology and quick results, education can appear overwhelming by comparison.

Returning to school is a big risk. You might fail. You might succeed. Either way, education will irrevocably change your expectations and your way of looking at the world. That can be the scariest part of all.

Adjusting attitudes—giving up old ones to adopt new ones—requires personal questioning and sacrifice. Expanding into the unknown requires courage and perseverance.

How easily someone adjusts to returning to school depends on the student's philosophy toward education. Sir William Osler, a turn-of-the-century Canadian physician and educator, viewed education as a lifelong course, a journey of gathering information and developing self-understanding. For this kind of journey, students need full freedom to study and explore wholeheartedly.

When Jerome decided to return to school after ten successful years as a civil engineer, his wife asked, "School? *Again?* You already make good money. What are you trying to prove?" She didn't have a clue how important it was to Jerome that he learn, grow, and master new information for its own satisfaction. She had become complacent, was not a risk-taker, and didn't tolerate change very well. Jerome went on to school anyway, with little encouragement from his wife. Unfortunately, she missed out on sharing the joy of it all with him.

Osler talks about approaching student life with "humility and an honest heart." This will allow the student to be truly open to many teachers and other colleagues and allow them to process information while the soul develops wisdom. A great key to learning is listening; a sincere desire to learn keeps the ears and mind open. It naturally enriches the self.

The student, Osler notes, must begin with a steadfast intent—to stick with it. A student shouldn't expect to master everything perfectly. Instead, working steadily and thoroughly will develop powers of concentration.

A tongue-in-cheek definition of an expert is "one who knows more and more about less and less." While professionals frequently return to school to develop expertise, Osler advises the student to adopt a cosmopolitan view of life—a sense of the broader picture—while specializing in one particular area. Knowledge then becomes well integrated and more meaningful to the student and those with whom the student works.

"Split your time between books and [people]," Osler encourages. In his philosophy, professionals returning to school have the advantage of learning theory, then applying it to life and work experiences. Learning becomes a natural extension of work. Questions asked become more relevant, and theories studied become more germane.

Finally, Osler suggests the student see humor and goodness in even the dullest of tasks. A dull task can help develop insight and patience, in addition to technical skill.

Osler further advises his medical students that humility in one's calling or mission in life, awareness of weakness while searching for strength, and a sense of power and confidence while learning limitations and pride in one's past assure blessings far beyond those they expect.

Part II

Get Set . . .

Chapter 4

Understanding
Cultural Diversity

Cultural values play a key role in how you view the world
and how you learn to succeed in it. This chapter examines
"traditional" and "contemporary" cultural values and how
they affect your approach to work. While individual background, talents, and training contribute to each individual's
unique experiences, this conceptual framework provides a
base from which to begin understanding the differences—
subtle and striking—that minority professionals face, and the
assets they bring with them.

THE DILEMMA

The diagram on the following page shows a comparison between a set of "traditional" cultural values and a set of "con-

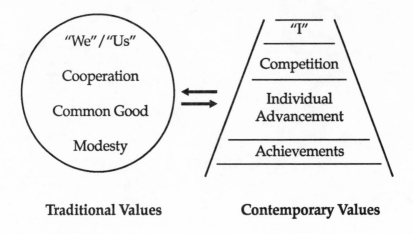

Traditional Values   **Contemporary Values**

temporary" cultural values. While you could argue that these values could apply to many groups of people, it's important to consider how it reflects your experiences, your upbringing, and your current attitudes toward home and work.

The list on the left shows a set of traditional values. The sense of "we" or "us" is crucial to this set of values. For example, when you're born into a Hispanic family, you're born into a group. The family is the core of survival and success. Ask a Hispanic living near his family what he's doing on the weekend, and he might tell you he's having a barbecue. Inquire about the guest list and you might get a vague answer. He doesn't need to issue formal invitations. Somehow, people will show up to eat, and there'll be enough food, too. Activities are not usually conducted alone or in a vacuum in a traditional culture. What "we" are going to do is often more important than what "I" want to do.

The contemporary culture, on the other hand, concerns itself with "I," with individual preferences and "doing your thing." The focus is on how "I" will get ahead, regardless of the cost.

Cooperation is central to a traditional culture, as typified by the circle in the diagram above. Anthropologist Carlos Velez describes the Mexican culture, for instance, as "mutualistic and reciprocal." If one member of the group helps another with child care, the other might return the favor by assisting with home repairs. The sharing or exchange of labor, money, and goods is often seen, even among professionals who have been raised traditionally.

Competition, on the other hand, is crucial in a contemporary culture. Getting ahead, and getting there quickly, matters. If you have help along the way, great. But you're mainly on your own.

In a traditional culture, the common good is considered important. How will it affect a family if a young Navajo moves hundreds of miles away from the reservation? Decisions are made with consideration of everyone else in the circle.

Individual advancement is the name of the game in a contemporary set of values. You do what you need to do to get ahead.

Modesty is a central value of traditional cultures. You can do well professionally, academically, and economically, but you don't need to tell everyone about it. When you return home, you'll resume the position you've always held there, even way-back-when. A Superior Court judge might still be "Inky" to the neighborhood gang. The family will remember the troubles their now-successful relative had while she was going through medical school. You might be enjoying where you are now, but don't forget where you came from.

In a contemporary culture, it's crucial to know how to toot your own horn. If *you* don't, no one else will. Get ahead by being noticed; that's the key.

The traditional set of cultural values promotes a continual interchange between people, as shown by the circle on the left. A contemporary culture promotes individualism (doing it on your own), illustrated by the ladder on the right. The arrow between the two indicates the tightrope that many minority professionals walk between the two cultures—balancing, choosing, weighing, deciding, and balancing again.

CROSS-CULTURAL CONFLICT
AND STRESS

The first time a person from a traditional background experiences the stress of cultural conflict is typically when he or she starts school. To come from a circle of exchange, talking, and sharing, to be forced into a mold of independent thinking, solitary work, and quiet attention is a dramatic transition for anyone, especially someone who is only five or six years old! No wonder teachers or supervisors who don't understand the traditional cultural experience become frustrated with the continual talking between minority students or employees! The traditional minorities are only doing what they've been doing for years—interacting—but it isn't always acceptable in a classroom or board room.

Competition and the contemporary set of values are introduced when the minority starts school. Team sports, academic requirements, and social organizations teach the child how to depend on himself to survive and get ahead. That's a far cry from the circle in which he's been raised.

The minority professional faces a stressful challenge each time she must walk between the two sets of values. Feeling perhaps more comfortable in one than the other, the minority professional might end up feeling as if she belongs fully to neither.

It might seem unnatural to speak up for yourself and get recognized, but if you don't do it, you'll never get ahead. It might matter to you as a minority professional how your career affects your extended family, but to the corporation, your dedication must lie with the company.

The hardest part for you may be the continual feeling you might experience of being alone, on your own, with loved ones out of reach and coworkers even more distant. But that's the price you have to pay. The challenge is to pick the best of both and minimize the cost.

ADVANTAGES OF BEING A MINORITY

The good news is that minority professionals bring a wonderful richness of personal experience and resources to the world of work. The Japanese have a tightly knit culture that promotes modesty, cooperation, and concern for others. They've gotten ahead in technical production because they have promoted the same concept on the job; the corporation becomes the family or circle in which the worker lives. The combination of technical expertise and good human relations results in well-made, highly competitive goods.

If minority professionals can combine their ability to get along well with others and promote cooperation and team-work while mastering the technical skills to compete and get ahead, they will be able to solve problems resourcefully, efficiently, and creatively. They will be at the cutting edge of managing a diverse work force in a dynamic economy. That's a position of strength.

Chapter 5

Practicing Discipline

Most people associate discipline with punishment and restriction of freedom. In another sense, however, discipline is the training of the mind, body, and spirit through instruction, exercise, and control. For all professionals, discipline is the key to personal and professional freedom and success. For minority professionals in particular, discipline ensures perseverance and clear thinking despite obstacles encountered along the way. Beyond that, it adds a dimension of deeper meaning and wisdom to life itself.

Although it is not always easy, discipline doesn't have to be dull. It requires a desire and willingness to go beyond the surface of everyday life to a deeper level within to find your *real* self. Discipline provides a journey of inward discovery.

BEGIN WITH STUDY

One of the first ways a person begins to develop discipline is through study. Sitting and paying attention for hours is tough when you're six years old; it's also tough when you're sixteen, twenty-six or sixty. At some point, a person must decide whether he or she will become a student in a deeper sense.

The true purpose of study is to teach you how to think. Study moves you from seeing to observing, from reading to reflecting. Literature and mathematics are no longer boring school requirements after school is completed. The true student learns to understand life differently through literature and appreciates the order and rhythm of the relationships between numbers.

In his book *Celebration of Discipline*, Richard Foster delineates four steps involved in study. The four steps are

□ repetition

□ concentration

□ comprehension

□ reflection

Beyond sheer memorization, *repetition* is the basis of understanding. As you are exposed to new information repeatedly over time, it begins to change how you think and live. *Concentration* is the second step. Focusing your attention and centering your mind make study easier and more efficient.

Comprehension and *reflection* follow. To understand what you're studying is comprehension; to see its significance comes through reflection. For example, a water-systems engineer can design efficient irrigation and pumping systems. That's comprehension of what is needed. To see how the misuse of water affects our lives now and in the future takes reflection. With that ability, the true student acquires a different sense of respect and responsibility for what he knows and what he must do.

Included in all four steps of study is yet another important and demanding component: *observation*. Many times you may have asked someone what he thought about another person's actions and discovered that he hadn't even noticed them. Sometimes you may have arrived at a destination but don't remember the route you took. Sometimes you can scarcely remember what you ate, who you saw, or what they said. These things happen because you failed to "observe" what was going on around you.

To increase your powers of observation, begin by observing nature. You'll find order in the midst of apparent randomness, simplicity amidst complexity, and variety amidst the sameness reflected throughout all of life. When you increase your powers of observation, you will increase the effectiveness of the four components of study. Your "study" will be deeper and more meaningful.

Minorities may not typically think about study as being a crucial aspect of success because they usually associate study with formal schooling, and their academic background might be limited. Viewed as a discipline, study puts even simple events into a new perspective.

"I don't understand office politics!" Sharlyne moaned. "They told me being black shouldn't matter, that it's office politics that makes the difference. But it feels just like exclusion anyway, mostly because I'm black. Of course, women don't do real well here, either. But I'm determined to make it. I know I can."

She did. Taking a new approach, Sharlyne decided to study the situation. She watched the company rules and roles and how people behaved. She made every interaction grist for the mill, learning and trying to comprehend how things worked. At last she understood the system; then she examined how she could fit into it. Through study she curbed her tendency to act impulsively, increased her tolerance level for frustration, and put things into perspective. Study helped bring calmness and light to Sharlyne's situation.

THE IMPORTANCE OF SOLITUDE

The more people develop their careers, friendships, and responsibilities, the greater their need for quiet and solitude. Ironically, some people are terrified of solitude. The blaring of a radio, the constant ringing of the telephone, and a jammed-packed calendar keep us from being alone. Yet solitude is what we want and need. So we buy a Walkman to be alone but blare the music directly into our ears. We go camping and take the mobile home, complete with VCR. Or we invite friends over for a quiet evening and end up detesting the idle conversation.

People sometimes avoid solitude because they confuse "being alone" with being "lonely." For many minorities, solitude is foreign. Reared in large or busy families where activity was plentiful but privacy and quiet time were scarce, they view constant commotion as the norm.

No matter what you might have learned to live with, constant commotion is exhausting. Solitude is important because it allows you to spend time with yourself and get to know yourself better. It allows time for your "battery," your source of energy, to "recharge." Solitude permits creativity to flow and problems to be resolved, and it allows the voice within you to guide you on things that matter.

To find solitude, silence is essential and listening is mandatory. Seek the quiet around you, then listen to the voice within. You may feel uneasy at first if all you hear are your anxieties, but you'll slowly begin to find a calmness. This is the source of your self-discovery.

Solitude does not mean isolating yourself from people. In fact, you can experience that inner calmness and sense of direction even in a crowd. You'll be able to separate yourself from what "they" believe so that you can listen to what you believe. Once you find solitude, the bottom line, production costs, and deadlines take on a new meaning. But you can't reach that point until you stop and listen.

You say you have too much to do and the kids are too demanding. Find solitude anyway. Take advantage of little opportunities. Wake up thirty minutes before everyone else, then think, meditate, or pray. Use time waiting in lines. Let your mind wander or explore during boring meetings and find out how the real you is doing.

Find a place to sequester yourself. A certain room at home, a corner in the garden, or your office before everyone arrives can all be havens. Explain to people that you don't want to be interrupted. Maybe they'll learn that solitude is a pretty good idea.

Try the following exercise to help you achieve or retain your solitude. On occasion, speak only when necessary. Speaking breaks the inner silence. If you choose your words wisely, you'll retain the steady calmness that solitude brings.

> Alberto rose high in local politics and was considered the voice of wisdom and vision in the Hispanic community. Non-Hispanic leaders also listened to him.
>
> "How do you do it?" an admiring political science student asked him.
>
> "Actually, I listen and gather information, then I go away and think. Those quiet times alone are the most productive."
>
> Alberto had been raised in a family of seven children where it was always active and noisy at home. As a boy, he found his retreat at the school football field. Long after the team had gone home, he sat alone quietly in the bleachers and thought. He learned to carve out the solitude he needed.

SUBMISSION AND SERVICE

For some time, society has acted as if submission were a weakness, a way in which people lose their dignity. While submission is sometimes viewed as a self-imposed ball and chain, it can actually be a discipline that ensures freedom from always having to get your own way.

It's hard to give up control. Professionals, especially minority professionals, have often achieved despite the odds; they sometimes fall into the trap of believing they did it on their own. They believe that if they put their mind to it, they can control people, events, and things. Because they've sometimes been rewarded for it, they continue to act as if their power to control were constant. When they don't get their way, they fuss, fume, rant and rave, or turn inward, blaming themselves and bringing on depression or at least a bad attack of low self-esteem.

Submission is the discipline required to see the difference between real problems and self-will. It is a sign of growth to decipher what is truly important.

One of the keys to practicing submission effectively is how you view other people. If you can set aside your own ego and consider others as valuable, you submit to seeing the worth in yourself and others. You keep the positive and let go of the negative.

To listen and attend to family, friends, coworkers, and the community is an act of submission. It is particularly difficult to set aside your will with people you dislike or with whom you disagree. That's when discipline becomes even more important. To listen to an unhappy spouse, to uplift a discouraged child, or to take orders from an insecure boss requires discipline.

Submission does have its limits; when it becomes destructive, it is no longer a discipline of growth. But in general, you will grow personally and professionally when you submit instead of command.

The discipline of service is crucial for professionals to mature more fully. Minority professionals pay a debt of service to their communities in return for some of the advantages they experience or the benefits they receive through their work. Spoken or implied messages state, "Don't forget where

you come from." These messages compel a minority professional to share the good with fellow minorities who have not
yet benefited. The discipline of service also promotes
humility.

> Carla was a successful stockbroker in a major national firm.
> Twice a month she worked in a shelter for the homeless,
> serving hot meals and cleaning the facility. "It reminds me,"
> she said, "that I'm just two or three paychecks away from the
> same situation these folks are in."

It's easy to be comfortable, complacent, and almost smug
about success. Service to others helps refocus your purpose. It
reminds you of the priorities and "basics" in life, such as family, love, and human respect. It also engenders gratitude—a
potent antidote against discouragement and arrogance.

The key to practicing service is to do it selflessly. That
means not expecting "just rewards," not worrying if people
will return the favor, not picking who is "worthy" of your
help, and not insisting on "helping." True service does the job
regardless of the task, the recipients, or the rewards. It heals
and nurtures the server and those served.

CORNERSTONE OF ALL
DISCIPLINE

The cornerstone of all the disciplines is humility. In many
professions it is often the hardest to find. How often have you
met someone who is a professional whiz but lacks the heart to
do any real good? What about the person who becomes ar-
rogant instead of being grateful for his achievements?

The challenge for *all* professionals is to cultivate their craft
with discipline and humility. Through study, you will find
knowledge and understanding. Through solitude, you will

find inner guidance. Submission and service will keep things in perspective. Humility will ensure objectivity, a clear sense of priorities, and the quiet satisfaction every professional deserves.

For minority professionals, discipline and humility are the keys to perseverance despite obstacles, flexibility when things don't go as planned, objectivity in the face of discouragement, and a clear mind that keeps you pointed in the right direction: forward.

Chapter 6

Learning to Ask

It's amazing what you can get in life if you ask. It's even more amazing what you can miss by not asking!

There are two major ways of going after what you want: creating an opportunity and seizing one. Both involve asking. Let's first examine how you can create an opportunity.

CREATING OPPORTUNITIES

It's usually a good idea to keep your eyes open for professional opportunities, even if you're content with your current work situation. If you're alert to the activity around you in your field, you'll be more apt to be at the right place at the right time when it comes to getting ahead. Adopt the philosophy that what you're doing now is only temporary. In time, another opportunity will present greater challenges, which you'll choose to meet.

With this philosophy, everything's fair game. Whether you're at professional meetings, business luncheons, cocktail parties, softball games, or even casually meeting someone as you go about your daily business, listen carefully to what they say. They may have information about something that interests you and holds potential for career development. Don't discard ideas too quickly. Give yourself time to assess a situation and examine its feasibility; then pursue it, if you desire.

> "My job is very stressful because it involves a lot of traveling," said Joan, "but one of the good things about all the travel is meeting people along the way. Yesterday I sat next to an older gentleman on the plane. I was reading my trade journal, and he noticed the title. He asked if I worked in that field. It turned out that he used to be the president of the largest manufacturing firm of its kind in the Midwest, and is now serving as its national consultant. Because we're in the same field, I talked to him about my interest in consulting. We exchanged cards, and he's going to call me next week with an idea he thinks might interest me. Isn't that great?"

Always keep your eyes open for possibilities. Think creatively; not all opportunities are neatly packaged. Then make your own opportunity by considering the options, talking it over with others, and seeing what will work.

Another way of creating an opportunity is to decide what you want to do, then go about finding different ways to do it.

> Jose knew he had always wanted to own his own business and be his own boss. For twelve years he worked as a warehouse manager, stocking large shipments of goods then overseeing their transport to distribution points. Forklifts, tons of merchandise, purchase orders, and processing requests were all part of Jose's routine.
>
> He kept his eyes open for ways of combining his past experience with new possibilities as an entrepreneur. A crisis arose in which the pallets used to ship inventory were in short supply. He noticed that he had been returning them to the company for years, but that his company was still charged for each pallet sent with every delivery of goods.

The pallets came from another city three hours away, and his company was always at the mercy of running short.

Eureka! Jose figured out a way to produce new pallets and rebuild old ones, supply them to local warehouses in the area, and supply new ones as necessary. The demand was there, and so was his desire to own his own business. With his knowledge of warehousing and his connections in manufacturing, he made a business plan. After securing money for a small minority business, he opened up shop.

Opportunities do not always present themselves in the ways you expect. That's why you need to pay very careful attention to the people around you, the work you do, and the business environment in which you live. You also need to keep focused on your goals and your mission in life so that you're always looking ahead and planning your next move. You never know when your opportunity will come. You need to recognize it—and seize it—when it does.

SEIZING THE MOMENT

Minority professionals are often reluctant to ask for what they want or need. Perhaps they weren't taught how. Perhaps they've tried before and been turned down and fear rejection. Very often they don't believe that what they want is a right, or you may believe it's not acceptable to ask.

The first step in learning how to ask for what you want is developing a sense of entitlement. Not a "You Owe Me!" attitude toward the world in general but a sense of "I am a valuable person worthy of receiving what I need and want." You deserve a stimulating job, fair compensation, good working conditions, equitable relationships with coworkers, and credit for a job well done. You also deserve good relationships with friends and family. In short, you deserve to lead a healthy, productive life. Now all you have to do is convince yourself.

Minority professionals often assume they don't need to ask for things because other people know or should know what they need. That's a bad assumption. Few people are good mind readers. Even if they were, they wouldn't do it often enough to meet your needs. Speak up, enlighten others, and remove all doubt about where you stand. If you let them know what you need and expect, they're more likely to help you achieve it.

Before you ask for something, ask yourself what the worst outcome could possibly be. Chances are it won't be a great deal worse than what you're getting now, unless you're treading on very sensitive political ground in the office. Otherwise, you probably have a lot to gain and relatively little to lose.

If you're still hesitant, check your ego. Sometimes pride or an inflated sense of self gets in the way of seeing and seizing a good opportunity.

Next you need to figure out when, where, and whom to ask. If possible, make your request to someone who has the power to grant it. Make sure you have his or her attention. If the person is preoccupied with something else, full attention won't be paid to your request. Ask if it's a good time to talk, then be brief, direct, and to the point.

If you don't get an answer right away (perhaps the person wants to consider what you've requested), ask when a decision will be made. Follow up at the appropriate time.

When the decision is made, if it's not what you had hoped, find out whether it's final. If you can negotiate some options, perhaps you can turn things into a win/win situation, where both of your needs are met. Learn when "no" means "no" and when there's room for bargaining. In the process, you might come up with better ideas than you had in the first place.

ASKING FOR A RAISE

People often fuss over asking for a pay raise and fear asking for one. You'll hear someone talking with their friends, coworkers, or spouse about their need to receive more money for their work; yet they hesitate to ask the employer for it. Maybe it's because they don't want to be rejected. Perhaps they don't want to be refused because then they'd believe the boss doesn't value them enough to spend the extra money. Sometimes minority professionals don't want to draw attention to themselves, and asking for a raise does just that.

Whatever the reason, if you've worked hard and been loyal, if your time and worth to the company are greater than what you're getting paid, it may be time to ask for a raise.

Start by gathering enough information. It's important to know many things before beginning negotiations on a salary adjustment. Have at hand

- your length of stay with the company

- the date of your last salary increase

- significant contributions you've made during your tenure with them

- your worth to other companies in the same area (the amount someone else is getting paid for the same work elsewhere).

Sometimes minority professionals possess special skills or have provided special services that merit compensation. Serving on personnel committees focusing on minority hiring, speaking a second language that is useful in working with customers and getting the job done more efficiently, drawing in key segments of the community that the company may not have included before—these all "count" when it comes to contributions you've made to the company.

Once you've gathered all the pertinent information, schedule a time you can talk with your supervisor or whomever is in the position to approve your request. Tell him you want to meet with him privately for a few minutes; you don't have to tell him specifically why. When you meet, be prepared, direct, and to the point. If he can't give you an immediate answer, find out when he can, then follow up. Thank him for his consideration. Then see what happens.

Carmen had worked for the same company for eight years. It had been three years since her last pay increase and she felt she deserved a raise. Every time she thought of requesting one, though, it didn't seem like a "feasible" time for the company. First there were budget cuts, then a hiring freeze, then a change in upper management. She knew that if she waited for perfect stability in the company before asking for a raise, she'd wait a long time. She watched carefully for the best possible time, then made her approach.

"Mr. Franklin," Carmen began, "thank you for taking time to see me this afternoon. I really appreciate it."

"Sure, Carmen, what's this all about?" he asked.

"You know, I've been with the company eight years and haven't had a pay increase for the last three. I really like my work here, and I think I've done well. I reorganized the customer service center, added bilingual services, and implemented all the new procedural changes there. So far, things seem to be running much more smoothly. Turnover is down in that area, and I think morale has improved. I've completed some extra courses at the university at night to help me in my job. I really want to be happy staying here. That's why I'm asking you for a raise."

"Carmen," he said, "you know how much we value you. I've been very pleased with your work all these years. I've always been able to count on you, and that means a lot. It's just that we're under the gun right now with the budget, and I'm just not sure we can give you any more than you're getting."

"Well, I'd appreciate your looking into it. I understand the budget situation here at work, and I know it's been going on for a long time. I also know my work has been good, and I deserve the compensation. When can you let me know definitely if it's possible?" she asked.

"Give me a couple of days, because I have to check with Finance, OK? I'll see what I can do," he said.

"That's all I can ask," Carmen said. "I really would appreciate anything you can do. Thanks for your time."

Two days later her supervisor called her into his office. "Well, Carmen, six percent is what we could squeeze out of Finance at this time. I know you're worth a whole lot more, but that's the best we could do for now. It'll be effective your next paycheck," Mr. Franklin told her.

"Thank you," said Carmen. "I appreciate your going to bat for me. Perhaps we can talk again in six or eight months and see how things are financially."

"That would be fine," Mr. Franklin said.

"I'll count on it," she told him. "Thanks again."

That afternoon, Carmen wrote her supervisor a note expressing her gratitude. Six months later she called for the review he had promised. Two months after that, her salary was brought into equitable range.

Asking for a raise is a sensitive issue because it forces the supervisor to give you direct feedback on your performance and to back it up with action. If you don't get the answer you want and it doesn't appear to be negotiable, be prepared to exercise other options, such as seeking a new job elsewhere, biting the bullet and staying where you are, or asking for other benefits, such as flexible hours or increased vacation time, in lieu of money.

Sometimes a company takes advantage of you and neglects to increase your salary if management senses you're unwilling to make a move. Find out what else is available in your area, then go for it. Once you convince yourself you're worth it, you may find something more suitable elsewhere.

Chapter 7

Paying the Price for Your Choices

Some people drive you nuts because they seem to get away with everything. Then there are the helpless ones who wait to be rescued: miraculously, the rescuer appears. There are those who find joy in life working frantically at the office for days or months on end, while others are fully content staying with the family at home.

Everything you choose in life has a price, and you must always pay. Professionals, who make choices every day, pay a price like anyone else. For minorities there can be some hidden costs.

WHEN THE GRASS LOOKS
GREENER

Carolina and Ida had been best friends for years, but when Ida married and Carolina didn't, things changed. When Ida and her husband hit a few rough spots in their relationship, or their children's misbehavior was annoying, Ida began to envy—and resent—Carolina.

"Lucky woman," Ida would think. "Cocktail parties, weekends out of town, board meetings, a wonderful wardrobe, someone who cleans her house and does her laundry. Look at me—I'm piled waist-deep in dirty diapers and too tired to even think of going out."

In the meantime, Carolina would check into a hotel room while she was away on business and feel sad that she had no one at home to "check in" with, no one to wonder if she arrived safely, no one to complain she wasn't home enough.

"Just once," she thought, "I'd like someone to object to my lifestyle and want me to be at home for them, someone to make all this worth doing." *She* wanted what *Ida* had.

In another example,

Bryan envied George's freedom on the job. Bryan had been a stable, salaried employee of a utility company and had risen in the ranks through the years. Slowly and steadily he had seen his responsibilities and paycheck at the plant increase. George had started an auto-parts supply service several years after Bryan started at the plant, and his business had really blossomed. George now took frequent hunting trips and wilderness expeditions instead of the short fishing trips he and Bryan had taken in the past. When Bryan looked at George's income, he became envious and resentful.

"I work just as hard as George does, but I can't go any higher in pay," Bryan lamented. "There's George, raking it in without a second thought. Some guys get all the breaks."

Look again.

Whenever the grass looks greener on the other side, check how much the "pasture" costs. Ida's price tag for the security of having a family was giving up the freedom to do as she pleased, where, when, and with whom. Carolina had the freedom, but she often ended up enjoying it alone. Bryan paid for his security with limited mobility on the job, while George paid for his "freedom" with increasing responsibility and greater financial risks.

Every choice in life has a price. Minority professionals seeking career success also pay.

Costs of Being a Minority Professional

The first costs usually incurred by ethnic minority professionals are education costs. If you were the first in your family to go to college, the first price you paid was in deciding to break the mold and do something different. If no one else was going to college, you eventually said goodbye (at least socially and perhaps emotionally) to those who didn't go. It also cost you if you received criticism or if doubt was expressed by those who had not done what you were setting out to do. You paid by garnering the strength to do it anyway, just for you. You paid those prices up front and you hadn't even set foot on campus!

Once at school, you had to make sure you stayed there. Money is often the biggest concern of ethnic minorities, who must often hold down a job while carrying a full class load. The price you probably paid was fatigue, less time to enjoy campus life fully, continued worry over finances, and a nagging feeling that you weren't doing complete justice to either school or work.

There are many hidden and up-front costs once minorities finish school and begin working. These costs go beyond time away from family, moving somewhere new to find work, and adjusting once there. Often a minority professional is "the only" one in a situation, and so is set apart, intentionally or not. (For more about being the "only," see chapter 10, page 89.)

As a professional, you may feel you're carving out your own sense of identity, feeling your way on your own because no one "like you" has every done it before. When you return home to family and friends, they may not always fully understand what you're facing so they can't offer the kind of support you need.

With time, other costs also mount, like sacrificing personal time to excel and work and complete commitments to the community. Or like continuing to forge ahead professionally—still alone—facing bigger risks each time, with no guarantee of support or appreciation from others.

THE PAYOFFS

Throughout this book, the costs of taking risks, being "the only," dealing with family, playing office politics, developing a sense of leadership, and making changes successfully are discussed.

Rewards make the price worth the effort. Those who "paid" for their education with foregone earnings and years of study have the self-satisfaction knowledge brings and a key to opportunities otherwise withheld. Those who have sacrificed personal time for career advancement relish the satisfaction of a job well done and, if they're lucky, some outside recognition, too.

For any minority professional, the price is high. You must decide whether you are willing to pay those up-front costs and risk confronting other, hidden costs. If you keep your eye on the pay-offs, the price won't seem as great. And if those pay-offs are your satisfaction and your sense of completing work that is important to you and others, you've received the greatest prize of all.

Chapter 8

A Question of Ethics

Kickbacks.

Deception.

Tampering with specifications.

"Forgetting" to tell the whole story.

Each situation presents a question of ethics—questions professionals can't afford to ignore.

It matters why and how things get accomplished on the job. Beyond technical competence, political savvy, and opportunities to get ahead lies the issue of values, the knowledge of why we make the choices we make, which is built upon a foundation of principle. Personal, legal, technical, and political ethics put into action our moral decisions about right or wrong.

Leroy was offered a deal that was "too good to refuse." He was president of the statewide chapter of a professional society for manufacturing, and he had many contacts throughout the state. His long-time friend, Mark, had just opened his own business in the field and wanted to build a clientele. He offered Leroy an opportunity to make five percent on every project he steered his way.

At first Leroy was stunned. He knew Mark was designing a kickback scheme, but Leroy could scarcely believe his old friend would do something so obviously unethical. Later, when Leroy figured out how much money was potentially involved, he was seething.

"First he assumes I'd stoop to such a thing, then he figures I'd do it in grand style! Why would he think I'd risk my livelihood and reputation, even if the money's good?" Leroy asked himself.

Not everyone would be that clear about the ethical aspects of the proposal. Leroy's position in the professional society made him a highly visible target for any activity, suspicious or otherwise. Less-prominent people are faced with questionable business "deals" every day. That's when the question of personal and professional ethics comes into play.

DIFFERENT ETHICAL PERSPECTIVES

Ethics must be viewed from various perspectives.

First, ethics serve as a guide for determining what is right or wrong, good or evil. Unlike a law, which simply tells you what is prohibited, ethics provide the principle that tells you why. For example, you could decide not to take office supplies home for personal use because you understand that supplies belong to the company, not because you might get caught.

Second, ethics are the guide that outlines the actions that are allowed or not allowed within a profession. The acceptability of lying to a client, even when it's for his own good, or of breaking client confidentiality are grounded in rules that may or may not be altered so that everyone comes out ahead.

Finally, ethics provide the standards for the virtue or traits a professional should cultivate to develop a strong sense of character and to live in a sound, directed way. How diligent you should be, how committed to your client's welfare, how much honesty, integrity, consideration, loyalty, and respect count are questions of sound, moral living that you, as a professional, need to face regularly.

Ethics guide professionals in their daily decision making. While you may not be fully aware of the reasons for making decisions, the issue of professional ethics becomes paramount when situations are not clear-cut, when the professional must rely on his best judgment.

WRESTLING TOWARD RESOLUTION

Resolving ethical dilemmas is seldom easy, but there are some assumptions and guidelines that can help you. First, you must understand that the morality involved in ethics is not simply a matter of convention. You don't do something "ethically" just because you've always done it that way. Instead of a knee-jerk reaction, ethical situations and dilemmas demand reflection and reasoned action.

Ethics go beyond simple laws. While the law permits certain actions, such as disloyalty and some forms of deception, morality does not. Ethics require more than civil obedience; they require following your conscience. Moral decisions don't always work in your favor immediately. Sometimes a decision based on principle can be a real personal inconvenience, and in some cases it requires considerable sacrifice.

Ethics go beyond economics. If you spend resources— financial, natural, or human—you must ask yourself whether you are spending them for the common good or on what makes the most "cents."

To decide what to do when the ethical shoe binds, listen to your intuition. If you are morally developed and have evolved a set of principles that governs your behavior at and away from work, an inner voice will let you know what feels right and what doesn't. People usually get into trouble when they ignore or discount that voice and act against their better judgment.

If you're still ambivalent about what to do, define the principles by which you will live. List the basic characteristics you require to deal in good faith with other people and where you'll draw the line with those who don't fit within those parameters. Decide what you require of yourself in the way of job performance and where you'll set limits with professional demands. Make a commitment to those personal traits that are most important to you, such as honesty, competence, respect, and loyalty.

Once the factors you need to consider are defined, you can call upon your intuition to deliver your first judgment. Use your principles to provide reason for your decision.

Weigh the consequences of each choice and ask yourself why you would choose that way (not which choice seems easiest or most profitable). If you know the reasons for your decision and they're congruent with everything you believe, you've reached resolution. If something still doesn't sit well with your conscience, refer to your principles and go with the decision that favors what is most important to you.

Project ahead to see if the decision will matter in six months, six years, or even sixty years. Will you be able to look at yourself in the mirror tomorrow? If not, you need to take another look at your decision. You'll have to live with the bottom line. Ethically, you can't afford a deficit.

SOME ETHICAL DILEMMAS

Ethical Dilemma #1

Juan had worked on the design of a major civil engineering project for the city government for over six months. As he was putting the finishing touches on the proposal before submitting it to his supervisor, Elliot, he was called into Elliot's office.

"Juan," Elliot said, "you've done a terrific job on these plans. But it's going to cost us a lot more than we're being paid, and we simply can't afford to go with the proposal as you're submitting it. I need you to make some modifications. Change the plans until you get them in line with my new specifications, so we can at least make a marginal profit. But do it quickly because the final plans have to get out this week."

"Elliot," Juan replied, "you know I've already designed it as economically and structurally sound as costs will bear. We can't afford to go cheaper without risking quality and safety."

"I know all that," said Elliot. "Just do it, Juan, and call me when you're done."

Stunned, Juan figured he had a few alternatives. He could refuse to follow orders, obey the mandate even though he knew the risks, resign, negotiate, or risk his job by reporting it to someone who could do something about it. After much thought, he returned and tried to convince Elliot he was wrong. Elliot refused, and Juan ultimately left the company.

Such ethical decisions in technical areas are especially weighty because of existing safety norms. The professional has enough knowledge to realize the dangerous consequences of tampering with and failing to meet minimally acceptable standards.

Ethical Dilemma #2

Less obvious but equally powerful forms of ethical dilemmas often arise in office politics. Sadira and Henry had worked together for years designing software for a major computer company. They had always been cordial and respectful toward each other, but they had never shared many details of their private lives. Henry had said enough for Sadira to conclude that he was in an unhappy marriage, but he never elaborated beyond the subtle hints.

One afternoon Henry begged out of work right after lunch, telling Sadira he would be out for a while. She knew he was going to spend the afternoon with his lover, but she made no comment. An hour later, Henry's wife, Anna, called looking for him. She was in a panic because their daughter had been in an accident and was being taken to the hospital. Before Sadira could ask for further details, Anna hung up the phone.

For the next few minutes, Sadira anguished over what she should do. If she called Henry at his lover's place, he would know she was aware of his affair. But if she didn't call and his daughter was seriously injured and really needed him, she wouldn't be able to live with her decision.

Politically, the safest route might be to plead ignorance of his whereabouts and hope his daughter had only suffered a few scratches or bruises. But Sadira had to decide whether the welfare of his daughter was more or less important than keeping peace with a coworker. She had to determine whether it was more difficult to live with pretending not to know about his affair or having him discover that she'd known about it all along.

Sadira decided to call Henry at his lover's apartment to advise him of the accident. While she felt relieved about conveying the important information, she worried about how she'd handle Henry in person.

The next morning, Henry asked Sadira to meet him in his office. "Sadira," he began, "I appreciated your calling me yesterday. My daughter was a bit bruised and very scared, but she's fine now. As for the phone call, I'd appreciate it if you didn't share it with anyone else."

"Of course not," Sadira responded. "I'm glad everything worked out well."

Enough said. Sadira knew better than to ask for details, and Henry drew the limits on how much he would disclose. Had he revealed more or been more anxious or aggressive, Sadira would have had to handle the situation differently.

Ethical Dilemma #3

Sometimes ethical dilemmas in office politics are tough because surviving on the job has a lot to do with getting along with others. You may not condone what others do, but you still have to work with them. The ethical decisions professionals make can also irreversibly affect their careers.

> Margaret needed a job. She and her husband lived in a small city and the pickings were slim. Finally, an opportunity opened up at the company where her husband worked. She was offered a position as an entry-level engineer on a government project. The problem—the project manufactured nuclear weapons, something Margaret had objected to for years.
>
> The choice was tough. Realistically, she needed the job to help support her family, and job opportunities in her area were scarce. Her husband did not share her strongly held opinions on this subject, and she respected him enough not to try to impose her values on him. But now the issue was facing her squarely. She was forced to re-examine her priorities and her values.
>
> Margaret carefully weighed her options and decided to accept the position, but set two provisions for herself. First, she would keep the job only until she could find another position in a non-defense industry. Second, she decided to dedicate a certain amount of time and money each month to working with peace groups. Within a few months, another opportunity opened and she moved on, keeping her community involvement active.

Ethical Dilemma #4

Minority professionals sometimes face decisions—and the ethics that bind them—that non-minorities don't face. Justine had always believed that the person who was technically most qualified for a position should be given the job. She also believed in integrating the work force, including more women in various positions within the company.

Justine was offered a promotion to the position she had always wanted, but she didn't feel she was technically prepared to assume the responsibilities. The personnel director and her direct supervisor encouraged her. They told her she could learn, and it would help their affirmative-action plan gain strength, too.

Justine had to decide whether her beliefs about technical competence would be outweighed by her social beliefs in equal opportunity. She also examined her own goals and the opportunities the company would provide. Social, professional, and personal goals and ethics were in conflict. All Justine wanted to do was make the right decision.

She needed more information before deciding. She met with her prospective supervisor and questioned him about the responsibilities she would face if she accepted the job. She discussed her concerns with him, and he reassured her that her basic skills were adequate. Together they devised a plan for on-the-job and more formal training for Justine.

In actively addressing her concerns and developing alternatives, Justine created a win/win situation. The needs of both parties were met.

Ethical Dilemma #5

Pablo was tired of seeing minorities stifled in their jobs, unable to get ahead within the corporation. When he was promoted to supervisor, he was suddenly faced with an ethical dilemma: promote a minority coworker, a long-time friend and employee of the company, or choose the next person in line on the basis of seniority.

Pablo carefully evaluated both candidates. Technically, the senior employee was the most qualified, so he promoted him. At the same time, Pablo developed a plan for minority staff development. He plotted a progressive path of tasks and skills for minority workers to follow to qualify for promotion. He also watched as the management team promoted others, reminding, encouraging, and pushing for the advancement of minorities.

Professional ethics. Social concerns. Personal preferences. They must all be congruent for decisions to be sound and comfortable.

Part III

Go!

Chapter 9

All the Right Moves

Mistakes on the job are seldom fatal, but they can be costly. While some mistakes are obvious, others are more subtle. Not all are irreparable, but each one has its consequences.

Avoid making the following common mistakes, and you'll avoid sabotaging your career.

Mistake #1

Prepare inadequately, perform inconsistently, and fail to follow through on assignments.

People often mistakenly believe that once they finish school, they're prepared for a career. School is a place to learn how to ask the right questions and search for meaningful answers.

> The ink was hardly dry on Chris's diploma when he reported to work as a strategic planner. He knew the theories of urban planning, the methods for projecting growth, and

the formulas for calculating population density, costs, and system load. Within the first month on the job, he knew what school *hadn't* taught him—what to do if data weren't available, how to work within a restricted budget and how to deal with constituents who had personal stakes in how things were done.

Realizing that he wouldn't survive six months on the job at the rate he was going, Chris found a couple of mentors. One was an expert in applications and another showed him "the ropes" of corporate politics and helped him develop his skills of persuasion. Within a year he was on steadier ground and was being recognized for his efforts.

Technical preparation is an ongoing process that combines theoretical knowledge with practical application. When professionals fail to master or keep up with the knowledge in their fields, or the ways to apply that knowledge, they are technically unprepared. Chris was wise. He knew what he knew and what he didn't know. If a professional is aware, he will prepare technically to succeed.

Inconsistency in performance and failure to follow through on assignments can cause irreparable career damage. Your knowledge and potential won't matter if people can't count on you. A reputation as an unreliable colleague is a hard one to shake.

Mistake #2

View your professional position only in terms of personal gain, and fail to consider your personal contribution to the company.

Work around someone who feels as if the world owes him a living, spend time with someone who is concerned only with what she can receive, try to be a team player with someone who is worried only about the bottom line, and you're assured frustration.

Few attitudes are as limiting as an inflated sense of entitlement. Once an employer determines that a professional is in the company only for personal gain, he or she will shut down further investment in that employee.

Most corporations do not believe that the company "owes" its employees a living. What it "owes" is good products or services to its customers. Although a conscientious employer is concerned about how the company treats its employees, he or she can turn their back on a professional who doesn't treat the company well.

> Fred had been in a minority recruitment position with a high-tech firm for three years. He showed up at work at 8:00 (never earlier, but sometimes later), took his one-hour lunch break (never less, but sometimes more) and left at 5:00 (sometimes earlier, never later). He complained that his boss didn't appreciate him, that he was poorly paid, and that the company didn't value him. Perhaps what he needed to review was how much he valued the company and what he had honestly invested in it.

Initiative and loyalty often reap the greatest professional rewards. Doing something for the good of all multiplies the good received by the individual. Rewards are not always monetary. Beyond a paycheck, the priceless payoffs of earning a living are self-respect and the respect of coworkers.

Mistake #3

Fail to develop strong communication skills.

Sometimes a professional has a great image and nothing more. Once she opens her mouth to speak, or the first time he writes a memo, the image is blown. Good communication skills are often remembered; bad ones are seldom forgiven.

There's an increased risk for any minority professional who fails to develop good speaking and writing skills. Those abilities tell people what you know, how clearly you think, and who you are. A minority who does not write or speak well furthers the stereotype of minorities as unprepared or less capable. Without good communication skills, your credibility is at stake.

> Lou did well initially as public relations director for a large manufacturing firm. He handled informal groups with ease. All it took was light conversation and a glib tongue. But when it came to making a formal speech, representing the company to an outside group, or writing a press release for general publication, Lou was sunk. He couldn't present an idea logically from beginning to end. His thoughts were scattered and his reasoning was shaky. His writing only confirmed his inability to think clearly, group his ideas cohesively, and persuade others effectively. The "uhs" and "you knows" in his speeches were surpassed only by the poor grammar, misspelled words and incorrect punctuation in his writing.

When it comes to communicating any idea effectively, charm is not enough. Speaking and writing coherently tell all.

Mistake #4

Assume that if you're a minority professional, other minorities will take care of you.

Few assumptions are more dangerous or further from the truth. Sometimes there is an unspoken brotherhood between minorities. The backgrounds, experiences, struggles, and triumphs of minority professionals are often similar. But don't assume that someone else's investment in your success is equal to your own. Regardless of perceived or real kinship, people still fend primarily for themselves.

> After five years as the only minority in a small accounting firm, Joe took a new position in a minority-held firm. At his interview he felt at home, welcomed as "one of the guys." He was included in some discussions of company plans and invited to dinner with key managers. He figured that if the interview flowed that smoothly, working there would be a

breeze. "Finally," he thought, "I'll have the help and support of minority colleagues on my way to the top."

He was wrong. When Joe faced his first big political battle trying to sell a new idea to upper management, he found himself on his own. Though fellow minorities were friendly, they kept quiet when their positions were at risk. Those who would have been bypassed by it actually worked to block Joe's promotion.

Just because colleagues (minority or not) play back-up for you on the company softball team does not mean they will back you up in the boardroom. Ultimately, you're on your own. Make friends and engender support, but rely on yourself.

Mistake #5

Select only one mentor, then place unrealistic expectations on him or her.

Do that and you're bound to be disappointed. One person can't possibly be teacher, confessor, colleague, friend, and boss, so don't expect it from anyone.

First, you can't get close to a person who's on a pedestal. When one person is treated like an idol in a relationship, the other is placed in an inferior position. Second, heavy expectations bog a relationship down. Viewing someone as perfect blinds you to that person's human side. Yet it's that human side from which successful people gather strength and build wisdom.

If you adore and revere someone rather than simply admiring and learning from her, you risk missing the essence of what has made her special in the first place. If she disappoints you, and she inevitably will, you run the risk of rejecting her altogether, good aspects and all.

Sylvia looked at Janice with awe. Janice could speak well, write with impact, organize groups of people, and handle large budgets. Sylvia shadowed her for a year before she started to view Janice realistically. Sylvia found that Janice's personal life was shaky. Janice was afraid of being close to people and being hurt as she had been in the past, so she worked; that's about all she did. Conversations centered on work, "free" time was spent working, and friendships were formed exclusively with people associated with her job.

At first Sylvia was disillusioned. Later she was able to see Janice as a loving, intelligent workaholic who wanted to protect herself from other people. It didn't detract from Sylvia's ideas about Janice's good qualities; it simply put them into perspective. It didn't destroy the relationship; it equalized it.

Mistake #6

Speak up when you shouldn't and fail to speak up when you should.

Dallas always had something to say about things at work, especially when they were none of his concern. He wrote memos about the company phone system, the parking lot attendant, the payroll distribution process, the Christmas party, the annual leave accrual policy, and any other inconsequential peeve he held.

When he was passed over for a promotion for the third time, Dallas said nothing, and people noticed. Upper management didn't question why he spoke up about things that didn't matter and kept silent about issues that counted. They simply acted as if he were inconsequential. If you act as if it's no big deal, you will be treated accordingly.

Alternately, indiscriminate outspokenness can be risky. When you speak up about every little thing, then go to bat on an important issue, people may react as if you're "crying wolf." What you say is viewed as less valuable simply because you talk too much.

Pick your issues wisely. Don't sweat the small stuff— most things are "small stuff." When something is big, people will listen more willingly because they know you have something important to say.

Mistake #7

View issues only as minority issues, not as human ones.

> Manuel took to the stump every time a position where he
> worked was filled by a non-minority professional. He wrote
> memos to the board, talked it up in the lunchroom, and
> scheduled appointments with the plant manager to talk
> about the "minority issue."
> He missed the boat.

Non-proportional hiring practices are not only a minority
problem, they are also a company problem. That Hispanics,
blacks, women, and other minorities aren't hired is one thing.
That the company is propelling itself backward and exclud-
ing itself from a huge sector of the market is another issue.

But Manuel didn't see it that way and neither did the
company. They only saw him counting quotas, and they quit
listening shortly after he started talking.

Mistake #8

Confide in the wrong people.

> In the division of one company, the communication system was
> "telephone, telegraph and tell Anna." Any information you
> wanted spread widely and quickly was best told to Anna, be-
> cause you could be sure by noon she'd let everyone know.
> Maria was unaware of Anna's broadcast capabilities.
> Anna had befriended Maria when Maria first arrived in the
> division and when Maria was having personal problems,
> she confided in Anna. Next morning, Maria heard herself
> being discussed in the staff lounge. She knew that the only
> way they could have known about her problems was from
> Anna. But by then it was too late; her secrets couldn't be
> retrieved.

If you're new in a work situation, be careful about confi-
dences until you know enough corporate history to determine who is aligned with whom and whom you can trust.

Those too eager to listen and "get to know you" are often those eager to talk. Until you're sure, keep it to yourself.

Mistake #9

Isolate yourself when the going gets tough.

When there are only a few minority professionals in a work setting, the going sometimes gets rougher sooner. Sometimes people figure it's easier to keep to themselves. Although partially true, that attitude can be dangerous.

> Cal couldn't tolerate some of the office politics he saw, especially those of his immediate supervisor and two other colleagues. He watched them for a while, questioned it twice, then decided it wouldn't change and clammed up. Before he knew it, he wasn't invited to lunch with the others, didn't receive the office "scoop" as before, and failed to get memos informing him of important changes.
>
> Cal hadn't realized that by isolating himself from trouble he also ran the risk of excluding himself from the mainstream of the company. Being selective in whom you spend time with is important, but isolating yourself excessively is lonely and limiting. In fact, isolation might actually be *why* the going is rougher than anticipated.

Mistake #10

Demand more money when money isn't the issue.

> Dito always wanted a raise. The day after he got a raise, he wondered when he would get another one.
>
> Actually, Dito had been unhappy in his job for quite awhile. He couldn't advance any further without more education and he contended that he couldn't afford school. He felt the company was unresponsive to human needs and too concerned with the "bottom line." He felt unappreciated and stuck.
>
> Money wasn't really Dito's issue. Recognition and job challenges were his true concerns. Because he couldn't ad-

vance quickly and didn't receive much praise, he believed that at least he could ask for more money. Money may satisfy you for a while, but if it isn't the real problem, an increase in pay won't be enough. Try a change in what you do.

Mistake #11

Insist that a minority be hired, no matter what.

Rally the cry "Hire color or die!"

Sometimes the issue of competence gets lost in the rhetoric. Certainly if a minority is qualified, available, and willing, he or she should receive as fair a chance as any, if not some encouragement to help balance the work force. But if color alone is the criterion for hire, it's risky business for everyone.

> Sam was hired for an academic post after a lot of lobbying by minority groups on campus. He was a strong instructor, but he lagged in research. With time, his popularity ratings soared with students, but the rejections from journals kept coming. When it came time for tenure, Sam didn't make it. Despite appeals and protests, the committee upheld its decision to deny tenure.
>
> Sam really was a good teacher, but the position called for a strong researcher. The university supported those who published, and in their opinion, Sam's research was not strong enough.

Pushing a woman or a person of "color" into a position for which that person is unqualified is a disservice to the hiree, the employer, and the community at large. Hire color, but set everyone up to win.

EQUAL OPPORTUNITY FOR
MISTAKES

Every professional—whether a minority or not—has myriad ways at his or her disposal to sabotage his or her career. In many ways a minority professional has more than an equal opportunity; they have more chances to fail.

Because minority professionals are often scrutinized more closely, there are more opportunities for their performance to be faulted. Being aware of basic pitfalls can help a minority professional stand up to this critical "microscope" test.

You must keep an eye on your attitudes. Crucial mistakes that can sabotage your career often start with the way you think. If you're clear on what you're doing, if you know why you're doing it, if you have built your technical competence, and if you have a map of the "mine field" of mistakes that can be made, you'll be armed with what it takes to succeed.

Chapter 10

Being the "Only"

Whether it's age, gender, religion, size, profession, sexual preference, or color, being different is not always comfortable. Ask any woman entering a male-dominated profession, or ask an ethnic minority worker whose work place is not integrated. Ask anyone who has ever been "the only" and you'll find many challenges, restrictions, and problems in common. Understanding and identifying personal and group dynamics is important for "the only" or "the first" to succeed professionally.

> Janetta was the first black female engineer to be hired by a large aerodynamics corporation. For her first two months on the job, she was carefully observed by her coworkers. They watched whether she could do the job and whether she "acted like other black women." Even after time on the job, as new people entered the scene and other professional challenges arose, Janetta had to prove herself.

Rosabeth Moss Kanter, a researcher from Yale, notes that as a minority becomes known as a team player, she may become the spokesperson for that minority group or all minorities in the company. Task forces and special committees may see her as a representative in their group. If this involvement adds to her regular job requirements, fragmentation and burnout may result. If this participation is part of the job, overinvolvement in it may limit her chance to do the technical work for which she was hired. Either way, job performance suffers and the die is cast—"She hasn't got what it takes."

INSIDE OUTSIDERS

Being a pioneer can be both exhilarating and hazardous for a minority professional. He may get a lot of attention, but after a while his achievements may be taken for granted, while his mistakes get magnified. It can appear that his every move is watched. Two sets of performance standards may be established—one for all employees and one for minorities. In essence, the minority professional can end up working twice as hard to get half as far. He may become an overachiever, doing more faster and better than anyone else. He may be accepted, but at a much higher personal cost than his counterparts.

Sometimes minority professionals have the talent to rise high in the ranks of a corporation, but they choose to work behind the scenes instead. Avoid the hassle of the spotlight, they also gain little formal recognition for their work.

They will do well, but they will get no further unless they step into view and take the heat.

Janetta passed the initial phase of her new job but still felt like an outsider. She took up aerobics and metal sculpture, like other female engineers at the plant. She adopted their style of dress and became a fluent speaker of corporate jargon. She became part of the group by looking like everyone else, except for the color of her skin.

Kanter's research found that overachieving, blending in, and avoiding the spotlight are ways minorities survive if they are "good" or agreeable minority members. Those who question, stand apart, or speak out are labeled as rebels, malcontents, or radicals. Many minorities and women are taught to put others first and to remain docile. Being outspoken may relegate them to being permanent outsiders. Those who have "stepped out of bounds" on the job are often given the most difficult tasks and the least support. They may become scapegoats and receive blame unjustifiably. They simply have more chances to fail.

GROUP DYNAMICS

Group dynamics change when someone different enters a group. When a woman enters a group of men, the men become more of a group because of their gender. Contrast is introduced, and so is discomfort.

The lone Hispanic in a group of non-Hispanics, Josefina was often asked whether Hispanics like to do the things non-Hispanics do. As the only female and the only Hispanic, she received a double dose of scrutiny. Sometimes such questioning helps set people at ease; at other times it points out differences.

Attention to differences can make whomever is different withdraw. Taken to the extreme, the person can end up outside the professional network, receiving little or no information. On the other hand, if she's accepted as part of the majority group, people may conclude that she isn't the same as all the other minorities.

"You're not like Hispanic women, Josefina. You aren't overly emotional and you understand bottom-line business."

Compliment or not, such a statement shows that a minority woman can sometimes wind up belonging to neither group. The same thing can happen to a minority man if he has "broken the mold" and taken an unconventional route.

The pressure of being "the only" does not necessarily ease when another minority enters the group. Janetta had succeeded with coworkers and had adjusted to her work and lifestyle when eight months into her employment, another black female engineer was hired. No one had ever questioned congeniality among male engineers. But when Janetta and her new female coworker were seen together, the men commented about "those two" and speculated about their conversations.

It's often expected that all minorities will get along well together. When they don't, others may draw the conclusion that "they're always fighting among themselves, anyway," while disagreements among non-minorities might simply be considered "heated discussions."

DIFFERENT OPPORTUNITIES

While it may seem overwhelming, being different can actually be a winning situation for both parties. You must learn to accept the fact that you may never completely fit into any one niche. Being different can be an asset if you are comfortable with it and see it as an advantage. While there are no simple or complete answers, there are guidelines to consider when pursuing success.

Kanter's research on minority-group dynamics investigated opportunity and power as ways of achieving success if you are "an only" or "different." These are some of her observations.

□ An opportunity can largely be a state of mind or an outlook. Aim high. Envision the position you have and the one you want. Consider the alternatives in a situation and become a creative problem solver. For example, a woman notices the long line of people waiting as she stands for forty-five minutes to get license plates for her car. As she's waiting, she figures out a way to save people time and make herself a little money. For ten dollars, she'll do all your paperwork and even stand in line for you. For every obstacle, it's important to seek an innovative solution, a way of getting unstuck. Being different can actually give license for trying new things, if other people benefit.

- Jobs that promote autonomy and innovation are more resilient in times of financial hardship. Be committed, yet versatile. Do your work differently and more efficiently, and everybody wins.

- Professionals must avoid "low-ceiling" or dead-end jobs. Many women, especially minorities, have traditionally held lower-paying, short-ladder positions. Go the unknown route for greater advancement potential.

- It's important to be familiar with the routes into and out of positions where you work. People may dead-end in a position because their education or experience is too limited for more advancement. Ask someone in a position you would like to hold what it took to get there and what options exist. Then choose your route carefully and work at it every day.

- Power is essential for maintaining a position of advantage once you achieve it. Self-confidence is the most convincing advertising technique. If you truly believe you have the power to do something, others will also believe it.

- Play office politics effectively. Learn the formal and informal power structure, and respect it. Choose a mentor and build positive relationships with coworkers. These are crucial to support your professional development. Chapter 12, page 107, focuses on office politics, and chapter 14, page 135, focuses on selecting a mentor.

- Keep the corporate "big picture" in mind. Information about the company's overall plan can help you decide where your ideas best fit. It also makes the rest of the job more meaningful.

- When possible, do work that is crucial to the corporation, and do it visibly. If you're the one who solved the ten-year-old problem, take credit for it. If you don't take the credit, someone else will. Be counted as a team player who can also succeed independently.

- Choose your subordinates carefully. Select those who compensate for your weaknesses, have a similar attitude and a similar set of work values, and are committed to success. They will be important in building a successful professional team.

The key to being "the only" is to decide whether you want the situation to be an asset or a liability. You don't need to wear your minority status as if it were a flag, but you don't need to deny it, either. If you focus on your technical abilities and acknowledge the issues of being "the only," the ways in which you are different will eventually take a back seat.

EXPERIENCING DISCRIMINATION

Title VII of the Civil Rights Act of 1964 prohibits discrimination in hiring, promotion, compensation, and other conditions of employment based upon race, color, creed, gender, pregnancy, or national origin. Its original intent was to help ensure equal employment opportunities for all people. However, unfair treatment of different groups of people in the work place, disparate impacts of an employer's actions on different groups, and harassment still occur, subtle or not, even when the law is enforced.

The challenge minority professionals face is knowing when to recognize discrimination and how to handle it. Title VII and its ancillary laws spell out the legal grounds for taking action in cases of discrimination. Subtle discrimination is more pervasive and, for most minority professionals, tougher to tolerate.

The difficulty with subtle discrimination is that you can't always put your finger on it until it's over and you're left with the sting. Maybe it's based on your age, gender, sexual preference, religious beliefs, or political leanings. Perhaps it's because of your race or choice of friends. Sometimes the way you think, the position you hold, or what you represent might be the source.

Regardless of the reason (it's seldom rational), the purpose of discrimination is the same—to exclude. The roots are also usually the same—fear and ignorance.

Margie was thrilled with her promotion. She had worked long and hard for it and she felt she really deserved it. Her coworkers didn't agree. Shortly after she assumed her new job, she noticed they didn't invite her to lunch as often as before. She wasn't included in their celebrations and didn't get the company "scoop" any more. It bothered her a lot. Finally she asked one of the women in the group why she was being excluded.

"Well, Margie," her coworker responded haughtily, "we figured that because you're not one of us anymore, you wouldn't want to be included in our little old doings anymore, either!"

Margie was flabbergasted. She had never intentionally set herself above them, and she was shocked by their reaction. Their reaction was based on fear. They were afraid of being inferior, afraid of facing their own lack of progress, afraid of Margie changing, afraid of her becoming "an administrator."

In many cases, discrimination is based on ignorance, coupled with a fear of the unknown. People don't have to know anything about who is different, how or why; simply knowing a difference exists is sufficient. From there they can project onto the "different" person all kinds of negative attributes they either fear or possess themselves.

At other times people don't necessarily discriminate, but they are prejudiced against certain groups. They might not take specific action to treat these groups differently, but they do have preset opinions or biases against them, sometimes logical and sometimes illogical.

> Ramon and Millicent had been dating about a year when they decided to get married. Until that time, Millie's family had said little but had been anxious, fearing things would "get serious."
>
> When the couple announced their plans, her family told her she was making a terrible mistake. There had never been a racially mixed marriage in either family, and they feared there would be trouble. They "knew" Ramon would become a jealous, overbearing "macho" who would keep Millicent chained to the stove.
>
> His family wasn't much better. They figured Millie would be a spoiled, demanding snob who thought she was better than everyone else.

Both families feared the unknown. They had no knowledge or firsthand experience with how these "other people" would be, so they made judgments based on supposition.

DEALING WITH PREJUDICE AND DISCRIMINATION

If you're dealing with prejudice, at least there's some hope. If people have a preconceived notion of how a certain group will act or respond, you may be able to enlighten them about the reality of how the group behaves. If they're open to hearing it, you may persuade them before any actual discrimination occurs.

Discrimination is tough, because actions have been taken and you must deal with them. In some instances, if you're the focus of discrimination, you can choose to avoid the situation. In other cases, it must be dealt with. Unfortunately, if you confront fear, you often get more fear. Unless you have a strong legal case, the approach might need to be as subtle as the discrimination.

Setting out to teach them "a thing or two" seldom works because they might not be willing to learn. Persevering and dispelling their fears through action works slowly but more surely. As those who have discriminated come to see that you are safe and competent, you can get them to listen, if only a little.

Once you get by the differences to the similarities, the situation may ease. But don't expect miracles. Some people are very slow learners. If nothing else, you'll learn much about yourself.

When a subtle approach doesn't work and the discrimination continues, you might have to approach the subject directly. Depending on the political situation at work, the issue might be taken up directly with the person involved, with the supervisor, or with the equal opportunity officer in your office. The risk in direct confrontation with those who discriminate is that it might end up being your word against theirs, and they might win. If they do win, they could then retaliate and make things even worse. However, if you are vindicated, the person will at least be made aware that you feel the impact of their actions and that those actions are not acceptable.

In a situation in which you confront openly and are acknowledged, you can let people know what is appropriate, what the limits are, and what kind of treatment you'll accept from them. The tough judgment call for the victim of discrimination is to decide whether the confrontation is worth the possible grief it might incur and whether it will change the offender's behavior. In extreme cases of discrimination or harassment, you may feel you have to deal with the situation to defend yourself, maintain your dignity, and set appropriate limits with others.

In most cases, a minority professional ferrets out discrimination and prejudice intuitively. Just treatment is a right, and your intuition is worth listening to.

BEING BETRAYED BY "YOUR OWN"

Minorities often assume, when they work with members of the same minority, that the differential treatment they have experienced in the past will stop. Sometimes it does, but very often it doesn't. In fact, many minorities report that their biggest shock and the greatest offense is the poor treatment they receive from fellow minorities. Don't be surprised when women don't help women, when blacks turn the other way, when fellow Hispanics won't lend a helping hand. Even if you're prepared for such treatment, it's painful to be betrayed by "your own."

Some minority groups adopt the "old boys network" approach to defend and advance their own interests. When the minority group doesn't play by those "old boy" rules, minorities can be left to fend for themselves. If the minority professional assumes their minority counterparts will help them, they may find themselves left out in the cold, confused, frustrated, and disillusioned.

> Isabel had worked at two jobs. Both times she was the only Hispanic in the group. When she was offered a position with an agency headed by a Hispanic female, she jumped at the chance.

"This time it will be different," she told a friend. "Now I'll have someone who will mentor me, someone I can count on, someone who will understand. After all those years of being the different one at school and work, now I'll feel at home and things will be easier."

To her dismay, things were even tougher than in the previous two positions. At first Isabel couldn't put her finger on it. Finally she realized that the Hispanic female boss was placing higher demands on her and being more critical of her than she was with the non-Hispanics in the agency. Isabel tried different approaches to building rapport with the boss, but she never succeeded.

One day, in a moment of weakness, the boss admitted to Isabel, "You know, Isabel, I've always felt jealous of you. You come from a good school and have great work experience. You're so articulate, and you write well. I always knew you would do better than me."

That's often the basis of being betrayed by members of your own group. While you assume they will help you get ahead, they're more fearful of staying stuck themselves. So they watch out for themselves—and for you, but not in a helpful way.

When they're not watching out for how you might gain on them, fellow minorities can be focused on getting ahead themselves. In some instances they've depended on themselves for so long that they continue their solitary journey to success. Unless they've developed a sense of helping the group move ahead as a whole, they're not likely to see that you need assistance and to offer it. When you ask them for help, they might respond to your request but not volunteer assistance beyond that.

Watch your assumptions when working with your own minority group. If you assume anything except the fact that you're on your own, you may be surprised and disappointed.

Check your own commitment to your group. You may not have been able to count on someone in your minority group who was there before you, but you can assist those coming up behind you. You can break the chain of non-support by offering it to someone else.

Chapter 11

Gaining Legitimacy & Recognition

When tackling the challenges of a new assignment or position, people often assume that good skills, determination, and dedication will ensure success on the job. Many initially enthusiastic employees operating under this assumption soon leave their positions, discouraged and bewildered at having achieved only moderate success in a job they were technically prepared to handle. Looking back they recognize that although they had the experience and skills to succeed in the assignment, they failed to win the confidence and support of colleagues. This support, often overlooked, is crucial to success on the job.

As the new human resources director of a growing company, Juanita was ready to tackle her new job with fresh ideas, energy, and commitment. Having doubled its size in the past year, the company was plagued by multiplying personnel problems. Policies had to be formulated and procedures needed to be implemented. Well trained and experienced in human resource development, Juanita approached the challenge with confidence.

In two months Juanita had studied the company and its goals, interviewed managers and staff, and presented her plan for the necessary changes in personnel. Her ideas were not as well received as she had hoped, but she decided it was because she was the "new kid on the block." She decided to implement the changes anyway.

In the following months, Juanita began to notice subtle resistance from others in the office. The work she submitted to be typed was returned late because other things had "taken priority." Upper-level managers greeted her ideas with skepticism. Midmanagers "hadn't had time" to read her correspondence.

The resistance became even more obvious when staff told her that the changes she had suggested wouldn't make a difference, despite the work she had put in. After more than a year of trying various approaches, Juanita resigned from her position feeling disappointed, tired, and angry.

GAINING LEGITIMACY

Gaining the support of superiors and colleagues adds legitimacy to a professional's standing. Legitimacy makes a person "official" or sanctioned. It tells others that the person has gained approval and should be listened to, respected, and followed. It's essential for success in any area that requires the support and cooperation of others, especially management. Legitimacy offers recognition. Without sanction, approval, or support, Juanita was not considered a team player by her colleagues. She was not empowered to do the task at hand, and it became an impossible one.

Women and minorities frequently face issues of nonrecognition, of not being considered legitimate or "official." An auto mechanic who believes that women are ignorant about cars may treat a female customer as if she can't understand the repairs for which she is being billed. The mother-in-law who feels that "no woman is good enough" for her son will find fault with her daughter-in-law's housekeeping, cooking, and child-rearing efforts. Minority employees who receive promotions may be discounted by people who believe that their colleagues got ahead for reasons other than competence— whether or not that is true.

ACHIEVING RECOGNITION

In the same way that a step-parent may feel like an outsider in his or her new home, new employees replacing well-regarded ones often meet with resistance. Their efforts might be greeted with "Joanna never did it that way when she was here," or "There will never be another production manager like John." Besides being new and unfamiliar to the group, the new employee may be viewed as a threat if he or she brings change to the organization.

Begin to achieve legitimacy and recognition by starting with your own credibility—your belief and confidence in your own abilities. Take the competitive edge by mastering some specific skills that will make you unique and valuable in the marketplace. Become an expert in that area, and people will look to you for direction. Being technically up-to-date is crucial for seizing a new opportunity. Building a firm, broad base of knowledge narrowing into an area of obvious expertise helps define your recognized professional role.

Performing duties not required by the job can help establish a professional's credibility, but only if it doesn't dilute that person's effectiveness in technical areas. Serving on committees or working on special projects can help you understand what's going on and can help you to be accepted by a work group. Being active in the professional community outside the corporate setting can also help bring credibility to you and your company.

Special-interest and minority groups may be worthy concerns of minority professionals, but it is important to be recognized by more general professional organizations as well. This is the way to become recognized and legitimized both inside and outside the corporation.

Concentrate on the future but keep an eye on the present. Set personal and professional goals and work toward them daily. Recognize your limitations, but don't allow self-doubt to erode your confidence. Self-doubts have filled the world with people whose fear stopped them from developing their full potential. If you're competent to do a job or fill a role, you must be the first to believe it. Once others see your confidence and your work, they'll be convinced about your abilities.

Listen carefully to superiors and colleagues. A careful listener learns much about others, including the corporation, while others learn that the listener cares, understands, and can be trusted.

Follow through on commitments, no matter how small. What is a low priority to one person may be very important to another; your credibility can be affected by a small "oversight."

Be clear about what you want, have a tentative plan for achieving it, and be patient. Legitimacy is not always granted overnight, so keep listening and learning while you're waiting.

COMMUNICATION IS ESSENTIAL

Clear, open communication is essential in achieving legitimacy. Unclear or distorted messages can lead to misperceptions and misunderstandings. State, clarify, and follow up on needs, expectations, and assignments on the job. If your abilities are questioned by others, you will have to make sure you are granted the autonomy and support you need to get the job done. This may require a frank talk about work styles and expectations with supervisors and colleagues. Setting realistic time frames for input and feedback are also important.

On the second day of Daniel's job as project manager, the employer was reviewing project goals and deadlines when he mentioned to Daniel that he would be reporting to Frank, another project manager.

Daniel had accepted the position with the understanding that he would report directly to the employer. During the meeting, he listened carefully and asked questions about the project goals. Then he questioned the chain of command and reminded the employer of their original agreement. The employer made the necessary change, and the meeting ended with roles and responsibilities being clarified. Daniel saw the project through to completion and is being considered for managing another major corporate project.

Gaining legitimacy and recognition is one of the cornerstones of professional success. If you build on a firm base of skill, credibility, and confidence, your other achievements will be firmly established as your career progresses.

Chapter 12

Managing Office Politics

Corporate policies and procedures are the formal, written ways in which businesses do things. Office politics is how things *really* get done at work. Professional survival requires mastery of both, but office politics is often the tougher of the two.

Unfortunately, there's no way to avoid office politics. The moment you get two or more people working together, politics enters the picture.

Professionals sometimes pride themselves on being "above it all," on not bowing to "corporate game playing." Although people at work do sometimes play games in which they maneuver or manipulate others, more often office politics involves understanding the way people interact in trying to get their jobs done and working from that understanding. If you look at it that way, office politics can be more approachable.

Minority professionals often face a complex overlay of factors in addition to routine office politics. Racial discrimination, sexism, favoritism, or exclusion often compound an already complex political situation at work.

The good news is that office politics can be managed. You can survive—and even get ahead—without sacrificing your integrity or your sanity.

MAKING A POLITICAL MAP

There are some things you can do to protect yourself. First, determine the lines of communication and the informal power structure in your business. Use a copy of the company's organizational chart to establish who holds formal power positions. Draw lines between the people on the chart to signify the kinds of relationships they have with each other. Use the following lines for different types of relationships:

> *solid line* to denote good communication.
> *dotted line* to show a relationship that is fair but not too strong.
> *slashed lines* to denote communication that has been cut off or people who don't get along.
> *bold line with arrows* to indicate people who are so close they're almost joined at the hip.

Draw in the lines between people at least two rows above you and two rows below you on the chart. When you're finished, you should have lines connecting each person to every other person at those levels.

The diagram on the following page illustrates the organizational chart and communication flow in a non-profit agency. A volunteer board of directors oversees Nan, the executive director. Jill and Dave report to Nan. Four

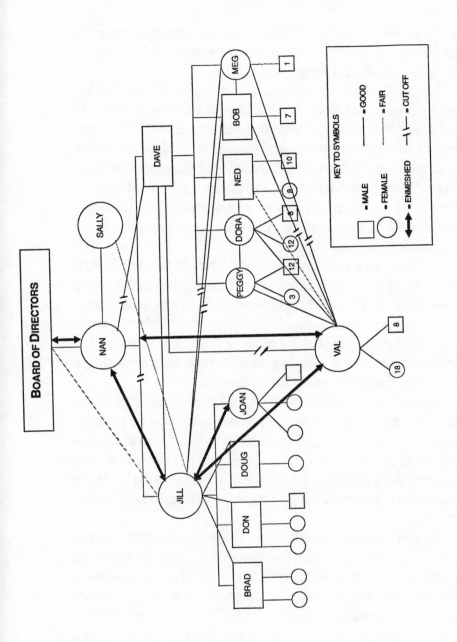

employees—Brad, Don, Doug and Joan—directly report to Jill. Reporting to Dave are six other employees, Val, Peggy, Dora, Ned, Bob, and Meg.

Without communication lines, it appears from this organizational chart that Nan has the formal power, with Jill and Dave second in command. Look again. With the communication lines drawn in, you can see that Jill and Val call a lot of the shots; Dave is on the "outs" with the power brokers. Dave doesn't even have Val's support, and any ideas that don't have Val's support don't fly. Meg and Bob are also disempowered and isolated because their communication is cut off from Val, Jill, and Nan.

You can draw communication lines between all staff members, if you desire. Sometimes the lines drawn vary from issue to issue. Those who get along well in one area of concern might fail to communicate about another. This process illustrates the dynamic nature of office politics. Use this tool to help you figure out what's going on now and what might happen in the future in certain areas of concern.

When you've drawn in all the communication lines, take note of who really holds the power, who has the greatest number of cut-off lines (and is most isolated), who has the bold lines between them, who appears to get along best with the greatest number of people, and who seems to be at the hub of the decision making (the person who makes or breaks an idea).

In your own work situation, determine where you are and where you want to be. Relationship lines on the chart will indicate areas of resistance. By studying what you have mapped, you can delineate a strategy for working your ideas through the people who hold formal and informal political power. Getting ahead isn't a matter of giving in or selling out. It's a matter of recognizing resistance and working with it, not against it.

For example, if you find that your boss's good ideas, and his attempts to promote your ideas, are consistently unsuccessful, check the communication lines between your boss and those who hold the real decision-making power. Check to see whether your boss has a tentative relationship with one or more of the kingpins. Maybe he's isolated because he's difficult to get along with. Perhaps he argued with or offended someone who is officially or unofficially "in charge."

See whether you can reroute your ideas to get them accepted. If the chain of command is important in your organization (it usually is), follow it while garnering support from the allies of those in the hierarchy. If you're wedded to the importance of your idea but not driven to get much credit for it, see whether you can convince one of the power wielders to share the idea. Chances of its acceptance will greatly improve. Just don't trample your boss in the process. Even if your boss is not seemingly very important, negative energy and feelings linger; negativity is politically dangerous.

INFLUENCING OTHERS AND DEALING WITH RESISTANCE

An initial step in planning a professional political strategy is to clarify your goal. You may have a specific idea of how you would like to see things done, but don't lock yourself into a strategy too early. Find out what others think of your general goal and get their ideas on how to go about it. You can figure out what their agendas are and what their objections will be.

Influencing someone to accept you or your idea requires that you try to understand the nature of resistance. Sometimes people adopt an argumentative style; they don't know any other way to relate to people. Sometimes a person has been dubbed "difficult." He or she feels and acts as if they must live up to that reputation and disagree because it's expected.

Alphonso was the procurement clerk in a large agency. He took his job so seriously that people swore he counted paper clips before they were distributed. He was known as the "Tough Guy," the one who managed the property as if it were his own. Actually, he was a simple family man who loved to do carpentry, but at work he "ran a tight ship." If you asked him for something, he'd question your request and might refuse it simply because he felt it was his role to do so. Somehow he felt he couldn't keep property under control and be less than tough at the same time.

People occasionally resist because they don't understand an idea and won't admit ignorance.

Katherine couldn't get off first base when presenting ideas to her boss. She'd barely begin explaining when she'd be cut short, corrected, or told, "We've never done it that way." The boss's real message was, "I don't know how to do it that way," but ignorance seemed to show weakness, so he opted for the "strength" of resistance instead.

Sometimes people object to get attention, believing it's the only way to get people to listen to them. At least disagreement might keep a conversation going! Still others say no just to "show who's boss." Logic doesn't matter; they're still in charge.

In some cases, people have other ideas or plans and decide that your plans must not interfere with theirs. This all-or-none, win-lose thinking surfaces frequently.

A resistant or difficult person is usually insecure. He may not like you because he feels threatened or unsure about you and your ideas or what could happen to him if you get your way. Maybe she feels she has always done more or better than you, even if she hasn't. Or you could be dealing with someone who is always critical and always has a "better way" to do things.

To get through to an insecure person, you must assuage his fears and enlist his help. You can subtly let him know, without being condescending, that you are as invested in the company's success as he is and that you're confident he will promote your idea. Focus on his strengths, minuscule as they may be. If anyone is clear on his weaknesses, he is (though he may not ever admit them), so don't remind him of them. Make things as safe as possible between the two of you. Politically, the more support you receive, the more power you'll have to get where you're going. In that way, everybody wins.

If it's too risky at your job to test your strategy, try a safer place. Practice dealing with resistance within your family. Figure out why someone doesn't agree with you and work with the situation until you have influenced him as you wish.

It's also helpful to have a professional network of people with whom you can safely share your ideas. Someone in the business world, but outside the corporation, can help you objectively assess a situation and the risks of your planned strategy.

FINDING A GUIDE OR MENTOR

A mentor can be a lifesaver. As a teacher, a mentor can guide you through decisions and seemingly inexplicable political situations at work. People typically think of a mentor as an older, godfather-type who eases a novice through a career obstacle course. In the book *Office Politics*, author Marilyn Kennedy describes various kinds of mentors who are helpful in different ways. Below is a discussion of five different types of mentors or guides..

Information Mentor

An *information mentor* keeps you posted on the inside scoop. He will teach you "the ropes" when you're new on the job.

It's better if the person does not have a direct working relationship with you so performance and rewards will not be questioned or compromised.

The secretary in the administrative area or the procurement officer may have been there the longest and seen the most, so listen carefully to them. Be sure to weigh any information they give you, because even the best-intentioned people have biases and can distort facts. Check things out with others, too. Information mentors are often well-respected and interact with many people, so treat them kindly. After all, information is power, and they are sharing theirs with you.

Competitive Mentor

A *competitive mentor* is someone who holds the same or a similar position as yours but not in the same corporation. Professional organizations are places to find these competitive mentors, who can tell you how other companies do things and how you can best get ahead. You need to be careful about those with whom you share company or personal secrets. Don't share anything you'll regret hearing if it comes back around the grapevine.

Peer Mentor

A *peer mentor* is a work-place teacher who holds the same or similar position to yours in the company. It's good to have this kind of mentor, but it can be dangerous if you end up competing with each other. A peer mentor is particularly helpful when you're new.

Once the power shifts in your direction, be sensitive to the peer mentor, or you could be sabotaged in your work.

Retiree Mentor

A *retiree mentor* is someone who retired from the corporation in good standing who will share information with you. This kind of mentor can add an historical perspective when you're weighing the risks of a new strategy or project. If the person has recently retired, his political information will be new. If he hasn't been around for a while, weigh the information against the current reality at work. Like a peer mentor, a retiree mentor has biases, so exercise caution.

Godfather Mentor

A *godfather mentor* is the kind you hear about—and wish for—most often. This person is typically in the company's decision-making hierarchy and is able to make things happen. You may seek him out or he may find you. The relationship with a godfather mentor is usually one of teacher-protege, with the godfather coaching the newcomer through challenging opportunities for growth that only a person in his position can present.

The advantage of a godfather mentor is that you may have the inside fast track to advancement in the company. The disadvantage is that if the political tide in the office shifts against your mentor, you might get swept away with it. If others view you as the boss's favorite, you'll also have to work harder for their acceptance.

Responsibilities to Your Mentor

There are responsibilities that go with having mentors if they have risked extending themselves by sharing information, encouragement, or opportunities with you. Most important, they deserve your loyalty.

As a professional develops, the role of the mentor changes, often diminishing in importance. As the professional outgrows the mentor, she can turn the relationship into a peer professional one or she can distance herself and move on. If the mentor is somewhat insecure or rigid in his thinking, the shift will be harder to make. Sometimes it's simpler to wean yourself slowly from the mentor and keep only the memories.

STAYING AHEAD

The real power in office politics is in *who* and *what* you know. To become an astute office politician, learn to listen and observe. Visit the cafeteria or staff lounge. Read memos and newsletters. Notice who socializes with whom, and attend a company ballgame or two. You'd be amazed at what you can learn through formal and informal channels. Ask questions and listen carefully to answers, but don't gossip. Rumor mongers get tagged quickly and bring about their own political demise. Showing genuine interest can win a lot of information and support from superiors and subordinates.

Do what you say you will. Nothing blows your credibility more than falling through on something that is important to someone else. If people know they can depend on you, you will be able to depend on them. This is not just politics, but good sense.

MINORITIES AND OFFICE POLITICS

For any professional, technical expertise is usually not enough to survive and get ahead in a career. For the minority professional, a working knowledge of office politics and a comfortable understanding and ability to play the game are crucial for withstanding normal group dynamics and the issues minorities face. Discrimination, being the "only" or token in the group, and being excluded (or included) inappropriately are easier to discern and handle when you can manage the office politics. Chapter 10 examines discrimination and tokenism; see page 89. If you learn to recognize these factors and can also understand the rest of the political moves at the office, you'll be able to strategize more successfully.

Many minorities have a difficult time making themselves politically astute at the office. Women sometimes think that only men can play the game. Ethnic minorities may feel overwhelmed or out of their league if they've never experienced anything like this before. Women and ethnic minority members often feel that playing the game to survive and get ahead is dishonest.

In reality, politics are everywhere—in the kitchen, in the bedroom, in the classroom, and in the boardroom. One of your first lessons in politics was when you began to learn how to get along with everyone else in the family. If you survived there, you can survive at the office. You need to know what you want and what you're willing to do to achieve it. If you have a clear sense of professional ethics, you can succeed in a system without selling your soul.

Office politics are not always brutal or wholly self-centered. Most of the time you'll work with people who are trying to secure or get ahead in their jobs. If you watch out for yourself, you'll feel less vulnerable against someone else's political moves on the job. If you consider that being an astute politician professionally is part of taking care of yourself and your career, you'll know you can get what you need in an honest way.

Grant yourself permission to develop your savvy about office politics. Information is power; the more you know and understand, the better position you'll be in to judge and decide what's best and what's next.

Chapter 13

Taking Risks

Some people are just plain lucky.

Or are they?

Some people believe that those who stay on the winning edge get all the breaks. Others believe it's who you know, not what you know, that counts. You may know someone who seems to breeze through life easily, enjoying success every step of the way.

Can minorities get ahead only through special programs and allocated opportunities?

Hardly.

Winning the lottery happens by chance, but few other events occur by luck alone. "Lucky" people are those open to new experiences, alert to seeing an opportunity when it presents itself, and willing to risk doing what it takes to succeed.

COSTS AND BENEFITS OF
TAKING A RISK

Most people view the costs of risk taking before they assess the benefits. Taking a risk *can* be costly. It's frightening. It's inconvenient. You'll have to deal with ambiguity. You might not be as popular as you had hoped to be. You could be embarrassed or lose your job if things don't work out well. Taking risks isn't cheap.

However, the rewards of risk taking are great. You might open the doors to new opportunities, opportunities you might not be presented with otherwise. People will look to you for leadership. Most important, you'll learn to overcome challenges that have previously stopped you, and you'll experience the self-satisfaction of pushing yourself just that much further every time.

Fear makes risk-taking difficult. Many minorities learn early to handle fear successfully at home, on the playground, or in the classroom. But if you haven't learned to handle fear *professionally*, it's the one thing that will make you take the safe road and get nowhere fast.

> After ten years in public relations and advertising with a major company, Graciela needed a change. She was tired of doing most of the work and getting little of the credit. She wanted the freedom to set her hours, select her work, and choose her coworkers. Calling the shots was what she wanted and needed to do. But she just couldn't seem to get herself moving.
>
> "I know exactly what I should do career-wise," she said. "I need to develop a network, manage my time, keep my priorities straight, and strike out on my own. I just haven't done it, at least not consistently. Sometimes it feels as if I'm frozen by fear."

That's not unusual.

Underlying any fear is a *lack of trust*—in your abilities, in other people and their reactions, and in the life plan that guides you. When you don't trust, you fear failure, dread disapproval or rejection, and even worry about handling success and all its responsibilities!

The tricky aspect of fear is that it feeds on itself; before you know it, you've worked yourself into a frenzy or you feel as though you've dug yourself into a hole that has smooth walls. Before the cycle of fear grips you and stops you from taking risks, review your attitudes and ideas about work and fear itself, then stop that cycle cold!

CHECK YOUR ASSUMPTIONS ABOUT FEAR

If you're afraid to take professional risks, you're not alone. To get a grip on the situation, start first by checking your assumptions.

False Assumption 1

Failure is bad.

You may have learned early in life that failure is "bad." Schools are great for teaching some students how to strive for success. However, for some minority students who don't fit into a certain mold or who fall between the cracks, school can provide experiences of failure. While failure is more common, success is valued more highly.

> Lincoln remembered his high school science project. While he had not been particularly good at science, he decided to put the school on the map with his attempt. No blacks had ever gone to the regional science fair competition from his school; he was going to be the first to try.
>
> He decided to research sickle cell anemia, reading all he could find about it in the local library. He described the dis-

ease on display charts and answered questions posed to him by judges. Months of preparation were evaluated in a few brief minutes, and Lincoln received an honorable mention. "Good research and presentation, but no new investigation or experimentation conducted. Nice try," the critique read.

"Nice try!" he thought. "All that work and all I get is an honorable mention? I don't even get to go to the regional fair!" With that, Lincoln judged himself a failure as a scientist . . . then and forever.

Success is often measured by income, possessions, awards, or recognition. When these criteria are used, minorities can appear to fare poorly. As long as minorities accept that definition of success, they'll continue to appear or feel as if they've failed (at worst) or gotten an unfair rap (at best).

False Assumption 2

Professional failure equals personal failure.

It's often hard to admit to failure because people assume that failure is the result of weakness or some kind of character flaw.

People often assume, for example, that failure is the result of poor judgment. Sometimes it is, but often it isn't.

When a business fails (often for reasons beyond someone's control), it doesn't mean the person behind the business is a failure. Unfortunately, because fewer minorities are in the professional ranks, all eyes are cast on their performance. If a minority succeeds, accomplishments may be wellnoted; then life goes on.

But a failure is seldom forgotten. People may not look carefully at "what it took" to succeed, but they will microscopically examine what went wrong—personally and technically. Somehow the pride of success seems less personal than the humiliation of defeat.

Janine was the first woman in her community to head a private engineering consulting firm. Dedicating herself to improved water quality, she tried to cultivate clients whose concerns were similar. After months of trying, she tore down her shingle, frustrated, angry, and disillusioned.

"I don't know what I did wrong," she lamented. "I did all the research I could think of, packaged my ideas well and worked at it every day. Still, too few clients. No recognition. No acceptance in the community. I guess I'm just not cut out to do this after all. I never could do anything right!"

Janine failed to account for the fact that the community didn't perceive a need for her services yet. A few more chemical spills in the water and another drought or two, then they'd listen. Meanwhile, Janine cast herself as a professional and personal misfit who had "failed."

False Assumption 3

You're either a success or you're not; success is "all-or-none."

Unfortunately, you don't often hear about partial successes. Instead you hear about fabulous victories and terrible failures. When it comes to achievement, coming "close" only counts in horseshoes and darts. Sometimes minorities who don't have a long history of success believe that getting ahead will somehow come easily and fully overnight. At the first sign of difficulty, they may back off.

Hector decided to run for the tribal council on the reservation. He hadn't agreed with the direction the government had been taking over the past few years, and he wanted to try and make a change. Petitions in hand, he soon met with skepticism. "You? Running?" some locals asked. "What difference can one person make anyway?" No experience. Looming, age-old problems within the tribe. Not enough money. Discouraged, Hector withdrew his bid for office.

When you assume that success is all-or-nothing, something born overnight, you miss the exuberance of getting better with each failure and each successive attempt. Progress is what really counts, and failure is the surest way to measure that.

False Assumption 4

You've got a lot to lose.

Sure you do. But you've also got a lot to gain. People often avoid taking risks because they fear they will lose, that their lives will be diminished, or there is more danger than opportunity in a commitment.

> Not so. Joaquin finally spoke up for himself on the job. After years of pulling major detail behind the scenes and getting little recognition, he finally squared off with himself.
>
> "What am I afraid of?" he asked himself in the mirror. "That they'll tell me no? That I won't get recognition? That nothing will change? That's exactly what I'm getting by not speaking up! I don't get support or the credit I deserve, and it's the same old thing. At worst they could fire me, but they have no grounds for that. I really have little to lose and much to gain—like a little respect—from them and from myself."

For every risk you take, there's a potential loss. Greater, though, are your chances for gain.

False Assumption 5

Success equals stability.

If anything, success means coping effectively with continual change. What outwardly appears to non-risk takers to be stability on the part of successful venturers is actually consistency in effort. Some people who haven't experienced significant success attribute someone else's success to luck. In reality, successful people simply try harder and more consistently, so they handle failure with greater aplomb and keep right on trying.

It may appear that opportunities come to such people more readily, but they don't. These risk takers are simply more apt to seize the moment.

> "Everything looks so easy for you, Neva," a neighbor commented. "Most black women have a terrible time getting ahead, but not you. You're able to sail on through like a duck in water. You really are lucky, you know. Most of us have too much going on to do what you've done. I'm glad things come so easy for you!"

Neva doesn't have it easier than her neighbor. It's her effort that counts! If you stop focusing on the liabilities of loss or change and understand that coping effectively with change is a key to success, you'll be able to see the benefits of taking repeated risks. That makes a new venture a little safer and more worthwhile.

False Assumption 6

I don't know how, so why try?

This is a great answer for anyone trying to avoid taking a risk. If people waited to "know everything" before they ventured into anything, nothing would ever get done!

Minority professionals often sense that they must know more than their non-minority counterparts to be considered equal. They often find themselves in situations in which they need to prove themselves repeatedly. But waiting until you know everything so a situation is "perfectly" safe will result in a long wait and little progress.

> Carol thought she would do just a bit more research before launching her new business. She had studied the market, learned about the product, and read reports predicting its future success. She took a class in sales and marketing, one in product innovation, and another in managing a small business.

"All I need is to take another course in personnel management, and I'll be set. That's apparently where most women business owners get in trouble, with the people they hire," she told her husband.

"What more can you learn?" her husband asked. "What you still lack you'll learn through experience. More schooling isn't what you need. Just take the plunge and do it!"

The point of risk taking is to learn. Allow yourself not to know everything, and go ahead.

False Assumption 7

I can't handle the responsibility success brings.

Sometimes people are afraid of succeeding because they believe it means they'll always be expected to do well in the future.

"I got the promotion," Alicia said, with dread in her voice. "They thought I did well on the project, so now they're assigning me a bigger one. I don't know if I can do it or not. And they're expecting me to do well this time, too. What if I don't? What if I can't?"

Actually, the chances of failing after you've been successful may not be significantly different than they were before. Your expectations for success may have been raised, so the possibility of failure seems more ominous.

False Assumption 8

Special treatment by employer helps me advance professionally.

Some employers who "protect" the minority from failure (or success), assigning safe work tasks, checking and double-checking the work, prohibiting or limiting mobility on the job or in the community, and granting special allowances for "minority performance" on the job.

"We're so pleased to have you with us in the lab, Ivy," the supervisor said. "You're the first woman ever to work directly in the lab, and we're sure things will work out well. I've submitted your name to the EEO Committee for Scientific Affairs; they'll be monitoring how all of us are doing in this area. Take your time starting on the projects ahead of you. I'll assign a coworker to help you learn the ropes and ensure you adjust well here. If things get too rough, just holler, and we'll make any changes you require."

This attitude doesn't help Ivy! When it comes to career success, safe *isn't* always the place to be.

STEPS TO INCREASE YOUR CONFIDENCE LEVEL

There are many things you can do to stop fear from intruding in your professional career. First you must realize that this is an area you need to work on. Then you must be willing to do something about the situation.

Below are some things you can do to help yourself take control of your professional life and begin taking some risks.

Examine any old messages and assumptions about success and risk taking that you've been holding on to. If these thoughts are irrational, they're probably keeping you from taking the risks success requires.

Now's your chance to change your thinking and rid yourself of your fears. Let's start with the assumptions we've just discussed. If you work to change these, you'll be on the road to success.

1. Failure isn't bad. It's an opportunity to learn and grow.

2. Failing professionally doesn't mean you're a failure personally. If anything, you've come out ahead by learning a lot about yourself and your business—quickly.

3. Success is not "all or none." Toss perfectionism out the window and let progress count. Successful ventures are built one step at a time, not overnight. Measure success in smaller steps, and risks will be easier to take.

4. Risk taking may involve some potential loss, but chances are you have more to gain than to lose. Weigh your options and decide. You know the old adage: "Nothing ventured, nothing gained."

5. Success is *not* synonymous with stability. If anything, it's a guarantee of continual change. If you realize that life itself is one change after another, taking professional risks that lead to change won't be as frightening.

6. It's hard to take a risk if you don't "know everything" before you take it. To help yourself over this hurdle, be sure you know enough, find someone who can help you compensate for your deficiencies, and then go ahead. The process of risk taking will teach you much of what you don't "know" anyway!

7. Not all responsibility comes at once, and you don't need to handle it all anyway. Success builds skills slowly. You still have the right to make mistakes. In fact, allowing yourself to be imperfect is a big step toward success.

8. Nobody "makes" you or "lets" you do anything.
   You choose what you want to do. While you may
   fear disappointing others if you fail, you'll
   probably find you are your own worst critic.

If you allow yourself to succeed and fail, you'll learn a great
deal and enjoy life much more. Go ahead—give it a try!

PRACTICE CONSCIOUS DECISION MAKING

Learn to Ask the Right Questions

If you don't ask the right questions, you won't have the cor-
rect information or reasons to help you determine what to do.
If you're having a difficult time taking risks, clarifying the
question will make taking the plunge a bit easier and safer.

Start by being honest with yourself. Cut through the "I
should . . . ," "I wish . . . " and "if only . . . " statements to those
that say "I need . . . " and "I want . . . "

Once you're clear on what you *need* and *want* and are
honest about what is actually happening, your options become obvious. Your decisions will be easier to make, and
risks will be easier to take.

> Nick had wanted to open his own business for years. He sur-
> veyed the market, read financial reports, investigated
> franchising, and spoke with other business owners. Despite
> all his information, he put off making an entrepreneurial
> commitment.
> "I just can't decide on what kind of business to open,"
> Nick would say. "I need to have those answers first."

Actually, Nick was avoiding the basic questions. He already had the survey information about what the market would bear. What he really needed to decide was whether he was willing to do what it took to run a business, regardless of whether or not he succeeded. Once he realized that the real question was one of his commitment to a new business, he knew that the kind of business he selected was really secondary. With clarity about his commitment and the proper marketing information, making his decision—and taking the risk—were easier.

Examine Your Options; Weigh the Consequences

Beyond asking the right questions in decision making and risk taking, you need to have a full knowledge of options and consequences. Once you know what the basic question is, examine your options. Weigh the potential outcomes and potential losses, then decide. If you've got the right information and are doing the right thing for the right reason, chances are your risks will pay off handsomely.

If Necessary, Use Plan B

Sometimes things don't work out as you planned. For those who aren't flexible, results can be devastating. It's crucial to keep your goal in mind, but it's just as important to remember that there are probably *several* ways it can be accomplished. For example, if you want to help people learn but being a classroom teacher isn't feasible, you could work in an adult-literacy program or lead a youth group instead.

Successful minority professionals are often accustomed to sticking firmly with their ideas, goals, and plans. It's easy to get thrown off balance when the unexpected happens and things go awry. "Plan B" is an essential alternate route on the road to success.

GRANT YOURSELF "PERMISSION"

Risk taking can be difficult enough, but people often put tremendous pressure on themselves with unrealistic expectations. These often stem from family messages about what you can and cannot do, what's proper, and what is expected of you by others. Some children grow up with a family message that they must be perfect. Other messages are that you must be self-sufficient or you can't be happy, leave the family, or be independent.

If you're being held back from taking risks by a feeling of not being "allowed" to do something, fearing that what you want to do "isn't right" or that somehow you're guilty of stepping out of line, check your family messages. Free yourself from the trap these messages set by granting yourself permission.

Grant Yourself Permission to Be Imperfect

For people who are driven, especially minorities, perfectionism and the need to be in control go hand-in-hand. But perfectionism doesn't guarantee that you'll feel you're in control. If anything, the harder you try to be perfect, the more you fear fouling things up! Let yourself off the perfectionism hook by granting yourself permission to be imperfect. It comes as a tremendous relief and can actually can help you relax enough to enjoy success and cope effectively with anything less.

Grant Yourself Permission to Learn

Taking a risk is taking a chance on learning. While things may not turn out as you planned, you can be sure you'll be smarter for the experience. Far greater is the risk of playing it safe and remaining stagnant!

Grant Yourself Permission to Ask for Help

Minority professionals are often accustomed to struggling on their own, of not having role models who are similar in background and experience to guide the way. Find someone you admire—regardless of ethnicity, gender, age, or persuasion—and learn that person's success story. Ask him or her to teach you the secrets of success, and you'll have someone rooting for you as you take those risks. You won't feel as alone in your new venture.

Grant Yourself Permission to Fail

This may be one of the biggest favors you can do for yourself. Minority professionals often live under a microscope, with coworkers and superiors watching their work performance to make sure they "fit in" and can do the job "right." While you may have to work twice as hard to go half as far, you still need to recognize that failure is a possibility and that you won't be doomed if it happens to you.

Oddly enough, people often get what they fear most. The minority professional who is extremely fearful of failing may build up so much tension on the job that his work performance suffers. If he overextends himself in the community and works unreasonably long hours to succeed, he may actually be setting himself up for failure.

Grant Yourself Permission to Succeed

It's generally expected that children will grow up and achieve, at least materially, a little more than their parents did. Many parents pride themselves on working two jobs or making other sacrifices so that their children will have opportunities they didn't have. Getting ahead in that way is expected and accepted.

For some minorities, the scene is different. Depending on where a person was raised, being ethnic and being poor are sometimes viewed as synonymous. The more you struggle, the more you share in the "blood" of the culture. As a minority professional who begins to succeed, you may fear that the "blood" will start to thin. Other minority-group members may look askance, wondering if you've "sold out," speculating whether you'll forget "where you came from," and fretting that, somehow, if you get more, they will get less. As a result, criticism or snide remarks may be leveled at you as you struggle in your profession. The "who do you think you are?" comments can cut to the quick and stop you dead in your tracks.

Success doesn't mean you're "less Hispanic," "less black," or "less feminine" than your counterparts. Some minority professionals might have trouble handling success. But you can give yourself permission to enjoy the best of both worlds—personally and professionally. You won't be "less"; you'll actually be "more"!

While some people can allow themselves to earn, own, and do more than their families, they also have a harder time allowing themselves to be *happier* than the rest of the family. If you do what it takes to do what you love, success and financial rewards will almost assuredly be yours. It's up to you to allow yourself to be happier than your loved ones. That's the true test of real success.

GO AHEAD ... RISK IT!

Without question, taking risks is often the best and *most difficult* thing to do. You can risk failure, humiliation, discouragement, financial loss, and fatigue. Benefits include increased learning, some advancement (despite any losses), and the satisfaction of knowing you tried something that was important to you—and perhaps succeeded.

If you look at your assumptions and revise those that need changing, review family messages that may have kept you back and "rewrite" them, you'll have a good shot at moving forward with confidence. You'll be able to enjoy success while, at the same time, remaining resilient about failure. You'll have the respect of others and, more important, you'll respect yourself for remaining loyal to what you believe is worthwhile—your future!

Weigh the costs and benefits of taking a risk. Chances are the losses won't be as great as you feared, and benefits will probably far exceed any you might have imagined.

Chapter 14

Answering the Call to Leadership

When I think of contemporary leaders, I think of Lee Iacocca, Eleanor Roosevelt, Peter Ueberroth, Henry Cisneros, Jesse Jackson, and my friend Nancy. Through appointed or assumed responsibility, each saw what needed to be done and accomplished it through others. While it sounds simple, it's not easy. Yet each of them accomplished what to others seemed impossible tasks. They did it with vision and conviction, inspiring others to believe in and dedicate themselves to supporting the cause with action.

We need leaders for more than the high-ranking, high-paying positions. We seek leadership in boardrooms and classrooms, leaders to lead our neighborhoods as well as our nation. For educated minorities in positions that can make a difference for others, the call to leadership has never been louder. The challenge is to answer that call.

LEADERSHIP STARTS WITH A VISION

A leader must be a visionary, able to see the overall picture and beyond. Planning for the next five years is important in business and your personal life, but seeing what lies ahead for a group or community is the gift—and the duty—of leaders. Chrysler Corporation's Lee Iacocca knew how to make a better car; he also knew what the future of the automobile industry would be and the challenges it would face. At a crucial moment in the history of Chrysler, he met the company's immediate needs while keeping his eye on its long-term survival.

The difference between leaders and idle dreamers is that leaders can motivate others to meet current and future challenges. They garner the commitment of individuals and shape them into a smoothly running team. The leader's vision becomes their vision. His or her energy fuels their actions. They willingly and enthusiastically do what has to be done because they believe in the goal and they believe in their leader.

LEADERSHIP—STEP BY STEP

A key strength in any leader is the ability to know her own shortcomings or weaknesses. To compensate for them, she will surround herself with people who are strong in those areas. This rounds out the group and allows people to operate from a position of strength and talent. Former President Jimmy Carter, one of our country's most formally educated presidents, may have failed in his administration because he did not surround himself with aides who had the skills he lacked. As a result, his weaknesses were compounded, making him appear incompetent.

Although leaders distinguish themselves by their particular style of leadership, all leaders share the ability to help others learn. Three kinds of leaders are often seen today.

Transitional leaders are leaders who excel in business. They are good at the daily operations of making things run and at accomplishing tasks. They may not be verbally inspirational, but they are strong, steady influences on those around them. They do a job well.

Someone who is knowledgeable and reliable is often looked to for guidance. *Transactional leaders* fill that need.

Transformational leaders help bring about greater, broadscale change. They help followers become leaders and move *current pacesetters* toward becoming *moral pacemakers*. Gandhi is still revered in India because of the changes he brought about for the people and because of his philosophy and practice of peaceful resistance. Transformational leaders guide, direct, and inspire.

In a corporate setting, young professionals often seek a transformational leader as a mentor. Some are lucky enough to find one. Whether close friends, bosses at work, or parish priests, *transformational leaders* appreciate and help cultivate your potential while influencing the way you think about life. They help raise the mediocre to the exceptional. The task at hand is transformed from a job to a mission.

FUNCTIONS OF LEADERSHIP

One of the main functions of leaders is to affirm values. A leader states the principles or ideas under which a group will operate, then carries out those principles in the group and in daily living. Leaders become more credible when people see that they believe and act according to principle on and off the job. To a true leader, a job is not simply a job, nor is a career simply a path to success. They are means of carrying out a mission and an opportunity to live principles actively.

Eleanor Roosevelt served the country as First Lady longer than any woman in United States history. Beyond that, she served as her husband's legs when he could not walk, spoke for thousands of people in need who could not speak for themselves, and helped to found the League of Nations. Now the United Nations, this organization still serves as the flagship of peace worldwide. Eleanor Roosevelt also lived her peacemaking principles at home while serving the nation.

Leaders set the agenda. They see what needs to be done, and do it. Often people will only sense or complain about a problem. Leaders state what must happen to rectify it.

Throughout the nation, neighborhoods have gained strength in determining the directions their communities will take. Historic preservation, planned growth, and water conservation don't happen because the general citizenry is conscientious. Leaders make people aware and convince them of the importance of taking a stand and acting on these issues.

Pacesetters motivate others. They key into people's hopes and dreams and help motivate them into action. Clean air, safe water, good schools, and a beautiful community are what most people want. Leaders let people know that these goals are theirs for the taking, if they will only commit and act.

Most important, leaders build unity. They are skilled in transcending personalities to stick to principles. They can motivate others, mediate conflict, and they can turn power struggles into cooperative ventures in which everybody wins. They make being a team player "the thing to do."

Peter Ueberroth faced a huge challenge in orchestrating the 1984 Olympics in Los Angeles. To begin with, he had to garner enough corporate and community support to finance the enormous cost of the games. He did this so successfully that the games showed a profit when they were over. He also helped the city mount a cleanup and hospitality campaign to enhance its image worldwide. Not only the athletes but Ueberroth as well came out heroes in the event.

Leaders have the foresight to train followers to meet the demands of the future. Current skills and approaches work now, but different ones will essential for future progress. Leaders educate people to look beyond the challenges at hand.

THE CHALLENGE TO MINORITIES

The challenges for leadership among minorities are complex and ever changing. The numbers of ethnic minorities are increasing at rates proportionately higher than non-minorities in this country. The resulting changes are sometimes dramatic, sometimes subtle, and always far-reaching.

Minority leaders must have a clear sense of themselves, of their communities, and of the world. They must avoid myopic views of the issues. Categorizing problems as "Hispanic" issues, "black" issues, "women's" issues or the issues of any other minority lessens their meaning and importance to anyone outside the group. The minority group leader must see issues as *human problems* affecting all people, even though they affect particular groups more than others. Even if a problem is local in nature, maintaining a closed, narrowly focused approach impedes progress toward a solution.

ROLES OF MINORITY LEADERS

Minority leaders have the challenge of stating the values of their group in relation to those of others. They must define and declare black values, Hispanic values, feminist values. They must articulate the understanding that equality and justice are human values.

Speaking around the nationl through the years, Henry Cisneros, former mayor of San Antonio, has shown that the Hispanic immigration problem in the United States is not one to be solved by quick-stop legislation. He understands the problem as one in which Mexicans want what all people want—the best for their children. As long as the discrepancy exists between what the United States has and what Mexico doesn't have, there will be an immigration problem. Cisneros states problems clearly, outlines an agenda everyone can understand, and makes each person question his own role in exploring the problem and finding a solution.

Minority leaders must define a problem objectively and accurately. Sometimes the group causes problems for itself; other times the problems are caused by those outside the group. Leaders need to assess where the problems lie and what needs to be done, then state both with conviction.

The ability to motivate others, convincing them of the importance of the task, and to teach people how to carry out the task is essential to leadership. Minority groups have long heard people tell them what the problems are, but few have helped them resolve problems.

Resolving problems requires unity, team building, or the formation of coalitions. It is the only way for leaders to achieve lasting, meaningful results. Trouble begins when one group competes against another instead of cooperating. Fighting over a small pie is futile; increasing the number of pies makes more sense.

Reverend Jesse Jackson has clearly stated the agenda of the Rainbow Coalition: unity and justice for people of all colors. He states values, motivates and inspires others by helping them see and use their talents, clarifies problems, and offers solutions. Then he tries to build coalitions to take action. When Jackson speaks, the passion of his mission rings clear, and each person understands his role in achieving it. While not everyone agrees with him, he makes people think and, if nothing else, causes them to ask questions.

Over the last decade, the plight of the homeless has become a national issue, a major blemish on the soul of America. Several years ago my friend Nancy saw homelessness as a problem in her community. (It still is.) She organized volunteers and opened a free soup kitchen near the downtown area, where most of the homeless congregate. Her service angered neighborhood residents, riled local merchants, and made city council members uncomfortable. Her life was threatened, but she continued. The soup kitchen was closed by order of the court, but she continued. She took her own money and received various grants to refurbish an old hotel to house the chronically mentally ill. She opened a shelter for homeless men and has included job training services for them. In everything she has done she has met many obstacles, but she persists.

Like national and world leaders, Nancy saw what needed to be done, and she's worked with people to do it. In spite of the obstacles, her sense of mission empowers her to persist. It is this same sense of mission that has brought other leaders to positions of national and world leadership.

ATTRIBUTES OF STRONG LEADERS

In addition to their tenacity, perhaps the most striking attribute of strong leaders at any level is humility. A leader's ability to maintain his or her humility influences the extent to which he or she stays in touch with the human side of issues. A healthy sense of humility is also at the heart of a leader's ability to stick to principles and to avoid becoming entangled in personality conflicts.

For the minority professional, an ongoing challenge is to meet the needs of the community while excelling in the work place. Corporations often select minority personnel to sit on special committees or to work on other projects, only to find that the time spent on these issues eats into the time spent on the job itself. As a result, minorities end up contributing much to the community life of an organization but fail to rise in its ranks because they're not recognized as technical leaders. Minority professionals must learn to balance those "inside" and "outside" activities on the job, making a mark on both.

Many people today believe we are facing a crisis; true leaders are becoming as scarce as some of our natural resources. At the same time, the opportunities for people of conviction to make a significant difference have never been greater. If you're one of those people who believes there is a way to solve some of the important issues facing your family, company, community, or country, step forward. Share your vision with others. You may be surprised to learn that others agree and will look to you to set the course of action.

Chapter 15

Rules, Roles, and Relationships—How You Get Along at Work

When Ernie left for work each morning, he carried his calculator, calendar, and project files with him. Although he didn't realize it, he also carried a part of his family history with him to the job. His father's drive, his mother's support, and his older brother's criticisms all played a part in the way he approached his work.

Everyone carries a cache of family history into personal and professional relationships. Each family and each corporation has unique rules, roles, and relationships by which they live. Understanding your role within the corporate culture or company "family" is essential to planning effective strategies for advancement within the work place.

Begin by looking at the rules in your own family. Determine who was in charge, how problems were solved, the ways people were included, excluded, or favored, and whether or not you were asked for input into family decisions. Now look at whether there are differences or similarities in the rules, roles, and relationships where you work. You can determine where you stand within the company.

EXAMINING THE RULES

Family and corporate rules are sometimes explicit, sometimes simply implied. "Always tell the truth," is often clearly stated and enforced in families. "Don't express your feelings" can be a rule at home that is never stated but strongly implied. Individuals are subtly discouraged from expressing fear, anger, or even love. People who grew up in a home with such an implied rule may be detached, quietly hostile or cautious when relating to their coworkers.

In corporations, explicit rules are "policies"; implied rules are "politics." Policies are important; politics are paramount. These explicit and implicit rules often conflict with each other. Family members and employees alike who follow the explicit rules but fail to understand the implied ones may become confused, frustrated, and eventually angry with the contradictions they face.

Ellie's family was affectionate and expressed their feelings openly. Family members were encouraged to ask questions and state objections. Shortly after Ellie began working for her employer, she noticed a few procedural problems. After asking a few questions, she approached the manager with her observations. She expected the same recognition for and response to her concerns at work that she received at home. Instead, she received a cool "Thanks, but don't worry," and was shunned thereafter. Believing a change was really needed, she kept appealing to an unresponsive manager.

144

Though she presented her appeal to others along the chain of command, no one seemed to listen and nothing changed.

Ellie became confused and frustrated with this company because it promoted itself as "a place where individuals are creative, management's door is always open, and staff input is appreciated." It was the open-door policy that had initially attracted her and made her feel at home. At first she didn't realize that the implied rules were different from those stated. Although the door was "open," the only input that was heeded was from those who were in agreement with management in the first place. Employees were expected to conform and to follow the company rules. Feelings were not to be discussed and questions were not to be asked. When some of Ellie's coworkers saw management's reaction to her concerns, they shunned her, figuring she was nothing but trouble.

Before making a move in the work place, look carefully at the explicit and implicit rules. They may be very different from the family in which you were raised. If the rules at home were comfortable and productive for you and those at work are not, chances are that the differences between the two sets of risks are drastic. If the rules at home, stated or unstated, were too restrictive and those at work somewhat less stringent, you might feel more comfortable on the job. Along with the rules, also examine roles, myths, and dynamics in the work place.

EXPLORING THE ROLES

Like rules, roles within a family can be explicit and stated or implicit and assumed. In some families, a parent who is afraid or incapable of making decisions may rely on the child to do so. In cases where a parent is an alcoholic or otherwise disabled, children often assume caretaking duties while the parent becomes more dependent.

Other roles assumed in a family include the rebel, the angel, the mascot, and the martyr. The *rebel* may be the person who opposes almost everything, if only for the sake of arguing, or one who strikes out on his own. Usually he's the nonconformist who is always questioning. The *angel* in the family can do no wrong and is much revered by the parents, much to the dismay of the other children in the family. Angels are not always included in sibling activities because of non-angels' resentment at the attention angels receive. Usually a family with an angel also has a devil, or rebel, in another person.

Mascots, also called *placaters*, work hard to please others and make the family happy. *Martyrs* make great sacrifices for the "good" of everyone else. They might bear their load in silence for a time, but occasionally they speak up to remind others of the burden they've borne. When unappreciated, martyrs become resentful and even more martyrlike.

Family roles can also be assigned or assumed according to a person's birth order. The oldest child is frequently driven and responsible, while the youngest, the "baby" of the family, might wait for others to take care of things for him.

The same cast of players can also appear within a company. The corporate "savior" might be the new genius who enters the job setting with all the answers to long-standing problems. These heroes are often admired from afar but remain distant from everyone else in the work place. The "lost child" in the family who says little at home will probably not speak up at work either. The angel at work is as special as the hero but may not be credited with possessing the same magical powers.

You'll never get a straight answer from a placater. Such a person tries to keep everyone in the corporation happy by agreeing with both management and labor. Placaters are the "pleasers," concerned with the social aspects of workers getting along. Managements positions are difficult for placaters because they hate to make a decision that might displease some of the people. They'll never forget the details of the company holiday party or summer picnic.

Corporate martyrs are not hard to find. They work long hours, skip lunch and vacations, and accept pay cuts for "the good" of the company. They remind others regularly of their sacrifices. They also question why others aren't as dedicated.

Compare your position and role in your family with your position and role at work. If the roles are the same, and if you were comfortable in that family role, then you are probably comfortable with your role at work. If they are the same but you were not comfortable with your home role, then a change through work might be indicated.

UNDERSTANDING RELATIONSHIPS

It's important to remember that families and companies are not all they appear to be, and that things within each system change. One company that had been heralded as the leader in the industry had drastically reduced its earnings. Its reputation continued to attract topnotch professionals, but new hires soon found that there was little evidence to support the company's mythical image. New ideas were squelched and employee turnover was high. Still, the myth of the company's strength prevailed, despite the corporation's failure to make an honest evaluation of its progress or growth.

Consider the adaptability and cohesion within your original family and current work group. If household routines and child-rearing were flexible, decisions negotiable, rules changeable, and roles loosely cast, you might expect that same flexibility in the work place.

Bryant was raised in a fairly structured family. Meals were served on schedule, household chores were divided and done regularly, and the house was kept in good order. Bryant knew in advance of his parents' plans, family activities, and his own obligations. He completed school assignments on time.

As a professional, Bryant worked as a designer in a creative engineering firm. Allowed to work as he pleased, he found it difficult to determine the overall corporate goals. No one seemed to know where anything was or what anyone else was doing. People frequently missed deadlines because they didn't know the deadline dates. When a deadline was discovered, other projects were halted and a crisis atmosphere took over as people hurried to meet the deadline.

Bryant found this frenetic work environment very uncomfortable. He missed the day-to-day companionship of coworkers because his colleagues worked alone unless rushing on a project. He finally left after realizing that he couldn't work in such a "chaotic" environment.

The way you grow up—rules, roles, myths, and dynamics—sets the stage for what you choose and how you fit into your work setting later. To understand better how you fit into your work place, observe the way people interact with each other, how they react to you, what spoken and unspoken rules prevail, and how close people are to each other. If you find any of these aspects of your work troublesome, chances are you had too much or too little of the same thing at home growing up.

Chapter 16

Dealing with
Difficult People

It's not uncommon that an otherwise perfect job is marred by having to put up with the pain-in-the-neck who works down the hall or the supervisor who doesn't give an inch. Most people have to brace themselves at least once in their careers against the braggart who just got assigned to their unit and can't do anything but criticize. Perhaps your marriage or other personal relationship is great except for those family members who persistently interfere. If it seems you just can't get away from difficult people, you're probably right. But you can learn to deal with them more effectively.

WHY PEOPLE ARE DIFFICULT

Adults, like children, usually misbehave for one of four reasons: *control, attention, revenge,* and *helplessness.* If someone

149

wants the upper hand in a situation, he may make things so difficult you'll be unable to do your work. If a person wants attention, she may recurrently make a major production out of the smallest assignment. The coworker who is angry at the company in general, or at you specifically, might get revenge by sabotaging your work efforts. One who doesn't want to work at all may feign helplessness in the face of even simple assignments, leaving you to rescue him from his responsibility.

Difficult people are not always aware of why they behave the way they do, but you can begin to get a handle on the situation by looking at the payoffs they receive in giving others a hard time. If a coworker has everyone dancing to his tune, you can be sure he's after control. If someone else garners a lot of attention for every crisis, you can bet crises will keep occurring. The practical joker who undermined the last project has revenge as his game. The sweet-talker who gets others to cover for her might seem helpless, but she really has everyone over a barrel.

If you can determine the payoffs, you'll learn what these people are after. Sometimes they're after more than one thing, such as control *and* attention, so don't limit the possibilities.

GETTING A HANDLE ON THE TOUGH ONES

Before you begin to interact directly with the difficult people in your life, ask yourself why they have the effect they have on you. Perhaps they remind you of someone from your past. Maybe they threaten something in your life, such as your security or your self-esteem. It may be they are running against the beliefs and values that are important to you.

Check your assumptions about dealing with people in general. If you have a strong need to be liked or believe that everyone needs to be happy or that everyone must agree, the chance is greater that you will be disturbed when dealing with difficult people. Once you determine which of your "buttons" is getting pushed, you'll be able to see that the difficulty is probably not so much with you as with the difficult person himself.

MAKING THE FIRST MOVE

The first step toward dealing with difficult people is to go with their resistance, not against it. If you oppose them, it will fuel their campaigns and make things worse instead of better. Once you agree with them, you take away the sense of power they get from arguing, and you can retain it for yourself. You will also get them to listen.

> Reuben was an Opponent. Whenever someone offered an opinion, he had to disagree. One day his supervisor presented a new operations manual for his review. After skimming the new work, Reuben said, "It'll never work. The procedures are unwieldy and no one will cooperate. Besides, it isn't clearly written. No one will be able to understand it . . ."
>
> Onto Reuben's oppositional style, the supervisor replied, "Reuben, you're right! A lot of time was spent on this manual, but the ideas do need more work. Go ahead and make whatever revisions you think are necessary, then get back to me. Then I'll take it to the committee. I'll need your revisions within three days, so get started and we'll talk later."
>
> The following morning Reuben returned to the supervisor's office, manual in hand. "I took another look at this, " he said, handing the book over, "and it really isn't that bad after all." When Reuben left his office, the boss skimmed the pages looking for changes. He couldn't find a single one.

Once you know the person is listening, listen carefully for emotions. Encourage her to express how she feels about something, and don't pass judgment on what she says. Instead, accept and acknowledge how she feels. It will bring her a little closer to being more reasonable with you.

> Mariana was the best secretary in the division, but after some scheduling changes took place, she began to complain and criticize management freely. Soon her complaints aroused tensions among the entire support staff, creating divisions between those who supported the plan and those who opposed it.
>
> "Mariana," her supervisor Lucilla began, "ever since we changed the work schedules, you've seemed irritable. I noticed you were assigned to night shift. How do you feel about it?"
>
> "Furious!" Mariana declared. "I had just signed up for a class at the community college, and now I have to work!"
>
> "I can understand your frustration and disappointment," Lucilla replied "Maybe we can work something out for next term."

Once you acknowledge how a difficult person feels (it may be the first time he becomes aware of his own feelings), listen carefully "between the lines" of his conversation. If he tries to build himself up, attacks others, or complains about things, he might be demanding attention or action, or revealing that he feels his life is out of control. Oddly enough, he might even be expressing love or affection, in an offhand way.

> "Martha is too much!" said Paul. "Did you see the way she organized the project plans? She made lists of every picky little task to be done, assigned someone to do it, and set a deadline for each one. She even listed the consequences if you don't comply! When I run a project, I never do all that stuff. I still can't believe they named her chief of this project. I thought I had done just fine. No wonder she never got married! Who would want to marry a drill sergeant?"

"Drill sergeant." Tune into what is really being said and you'll be in a position to turn things around by giving feedback. In this situation you could be objective and tell him how he's doing. Perhaps you could share your insights about what he's said and what you perceive is happening. Share how you see things and check back with the person to see if you're on target.

> "You sound upset that Martha was named chief of this project instead of you, Paul. Is she really that bad? Maybe you can learn how to be more organized by watching what she does. After all, you told me that, although your last performance review from management was excellent, they did indicate your management skills need sharpening."

By going with the resistance and not against it—why argue?—and acknowledging the person's emotions or helping him explore feelings that seem unclear, you can listen carefully for the real "meat" of the conversation. By giving feedback in a timely, productive way, you'll be able to move from the defensive position of protecting yourself against a difficult person to the offensive one of beginning to move things in a more positive direction.

OVERCOMING OPPOSITION

The next time someone disagrees with you, be aware that at least they're listening. You'll be able to tell how fully they've thought out their viewpoint and how committed they are to it just by determining how rational their objections are. A person who vehemently sticks to his guns, regardless of the facts, is probably opposing you irrationally. So is the person who does not respond to your feedback or the one who injects irrelevant information into an argument. The opponent who tries to make his viewpoint seem logical without the benefit of supporting facts will rationalize reasons to avoid budging from his position. The person who goes from objection to objection is probably opposing the idea simply for the sake of opposition.

If you determine that a person's objections merit some consideration, try to understand her concerns. Listen carefully to the facts—and feelings—about the issue. Let her know that you understand how she feels and offer some alternatives that might be more acceptable.

> "This budget is absolutely unacceptable!" Francisco raved. "Not one of our suggestions was included in the final version! How are we expected to complete our projects without resources? It seems like administration didn't even consider us a priority—we didn't get an extra nickel this year! This entire process stinks! We'll never be able to get our work done!"
>
> "Francisco," said John, "it sounds like your main concern is that your recommendations were not considered, or at least included in the final figures. I can see why you'd be upset, especially because you've worked so hard all year and are almost finished with your project. How would you feel if we either shifted funds from another area, sought monies elsewhere, or appealed the decision to get you some support for the coming year?"

By taking this position, you show that you have heard what was said. Now you've got the difficult person listening to you and considering some options.

Some people have an oppositional style of relating to others in general. If they're known as bullies or malcontents, chances are you won't be able to get them to agree. They'd sooner appear irrational than blow their image. Unless you have to work for them, you'd best leave well enough alone.

A real challenge for minorities is to be able to decipher rational opposition from racism or sexism. When you suspect the one of these is operating, listen carefully to what the person says and try to understand the objections. If they're irrational, you're probably dealing with prejudice—contempt without facts. If the objections seem rational, you may be able to pinpoint the underlying fear. You can educate the person and dispel any myths; allay the fear and gently guide the person in a new direction.

"We know you've usually hired all-male crews," the personnel director said, "and I know that as a supervisor you've had good luck with that practice. You sound concerned about a woman's ability to perform under pressure, and how she will get along with men. I'd like to assure you we've made important adjustments in our hiring procedures to make sure we are screening the best applicants. If you can give it a try for six months, we can review things and see what else needs to be changed."

Dealing with difficult people can be challenging, but it's a challenge you can usually manage. Acknowledging feelings, reiterating concerns, and offering alternatives can help improve the situation considerably for you and the person demonstrating a difficult attitude.

Chapter 17

Dual-Career Relationships—Trying to Have It All

Anita and Sal were the ideal couple. They had graduated from the same university—Anita in marketing and Sal in mechanical engineering. They had dated their last two years of college and married the summer after graduation. Five years later they had "done well"; they had expensive cars and a townhouse, took luxurious vacations, and owned a healthy stock portfolio. Friends and family were shocked when they separated.

"I don't know what happened," lamented Sal. "It seems we didn't spend time together or talk with each other much any more. Both of us were working. Before we knew it, our relationship fell apart."

The problems in relationships between two career people usually have little to do with decisions about housework, menus, or which movie to see. Relationships unravel because

157

of how people think, what they expect and value, and which assumptions and choices they make together. Often dual-career couples who try hardest to "have it all" end up with nothing—at least nothing that truly matters in the long run.

UNDERSTANDING
EXPECTATIONS

When male and female professionals involved in dual-career relationships were asked what they expected from their relationship, over half said they had never really thought much about it. Only one woman had explicitly discussed expectations with her partner. While some expected a lot of involvement and shared time with their partners, others wanted "freedom" and more limited family ties. Many expected equal sharing of responsibilities between partners; others had very traditional ideas of what roles men and women should play. Some expected an active family life with children; some wanted no children. Some wanted a mate to share their professional trials and triumphs, while others expected such concerns to be left at the office.

These expectations are not inherently good or bad. However, when a person's expectations are very different from their partner's, and differences have not been discussed and resolved, misunderstandings can result.

Rose and Bill didn't talk about money or career success much before they married. All they knew was that they were in love and wanted to be together. Rose worked as a personal-injury attorney in a prestigious law firm. Bill directed a local social service agency.

Soon after their marriage, career differences began to emerge. Rose was included in groups of private sector decision makers. Bill made his rounds of the United Way, always planning his next fund raising event. Both held community leadership positions that had seldom been held by blacks before.

Their greatest personal struggle as a couple was the difference in earning potential between them. While Bill appreciated Rose's earnings, he wasn't accustomed to the idea of a wife—especially *his* wife—earning more than her husband. Rose also had difficulty changing her concept of the "male as main breadwinner" to a *real* partnership in marriage.

Objectively, Rose and Bill knew they were fortunate to have the "problem" they faced. After talking at length about their mutual goals and priorities, they decided to change the way they measured of success. Instead of focusing on the size of the paycheck each brought home, they chose to focus on the contribution each made to their marriage. That placed the marriage on a more equal, comfortable footing.

This solution didn't erase the non-traditional aspect of the woman earning more money than the man in the relationship, but it did allow Bill and Rose to re-evaluate how they measured success. Their new approach relieved a lot of the pressure they had been feeling.

Consider the situation of Anita and Sal, in which expectations were not expressed.

"I remember when Anita and I were in school," Sal said. "She told me she wanted a modest career and time off to raise the children we planned to have. It's been five years now. She's been promoted three times and she's thinking about opening her own firm. I finally figured out we never would have children after all."

Anita said, "Sal tries to control me and tie me down. He doesn't understand how important my career is to me. He just wants me at home raising kids. What about my career? Would he give up his career if he were in my shoes?"

Anita and Sal started with expectations that were spoken, understood, and accepted. Changes were subtle, but this couple never reviewed or revised expectations they had set several years earlier. Sal still had the old ones in mind, but Anita had revised hers. They seemed miles apart.

To get their relationship back on track, Anita and Sal would have to look frankly at what they expected, what they wanted, and what they were willing to do to save their relationship. Then they would have to decide to do it.

ESTABLISHING PRIORITIES

In the case of Anita and Sal, they had to examine their situation and establish priorities. Sal was the second of three children. His older brother had been killed in an accident; his younger brother had died in infancy. His parents struggled to earn a living, so they never had much of a family life. In marrying Anita, he guaranteed himself he'd never be an "only" again. He had worked hard to get everything in order—a home, finances, and job security.

Anita was the third of six children. She had taken orders from older siblings and cared for younger ones for years. Her marriage to Sal was ideal; she could be close to someone, yet enjoy freedom and recognition away from home. Her career came first. Neither Anita nor Sal realized it, but each had made their top priority something they had missed as children. Anita sought adventure; Sal sought security.

With time, Sal began to believe Anita cared more about her job than she cared about him. Anita began to believe Sal was not as ambitious as she had once thought. She feared he would settle for the "dull family routine" she had known before. Until they sat down and talked, neither realized how important each of their priorities had become.

RESOLVING THE PROBLEM

To begin to resolve their problem, Anita and Sal had to decide first whether or not they wanted their relationship to continue. Both decided that the most important thing was to be together. Then they had to redefine what their relationship would be. It was difficult. For the first time they were consciously making choices individually and together. They had to weigh the options and accept the tradeoffs.

After a great deal of discussion, tough questioning, and some time apart, they decided they could have both a family and careers, but not exactly as they had originally envisioned things. Sal accepted that they would have a small family, not a large one. Anita would work at a more modest pace, have their first child, and continue her civic and professional activities. Sal agreed to help with child care and details around the house. Things didn't turn out exactly as they had planned, but they achieved their major goal—a good relationship with each other.

SETTING PRIORITIES FOR A SUCCESSFUL DUAL-CAREER RELATIONSHIP

There's a basic principle to success—you can have whatever you want. You just have to be very clear about *what* that is. Once you're clear about your greatest desire, you can avoid spending time, energy, emotions, and money on things that are less important.

In dual-career relationships, each partner must decide what he or she really wants. Then the two must work together toward a plan for achieving it. If both want a strong relationship, they need to make it a priority and do what it takes to build one.

"Not enough time for each other" was the most common complaint among dual-career couples interviewed.

"The business and 'busy-ness' took over our lives," reported one journalist. "Before we knew it, we forgot we wanted to grow and be together. We used to be like one spirit together. Then I noticed as we got more involved in other things, we started to grow apart."

Couples who have built successful relationships along with careers have decided that spending time together is a priority, and they stick to their priorities. Each person is more selective about extra work assignments, civic responsibilities, and other activities away from their relationship. It's a matter of choice. Do you want more business cocktail conversation, nine more holes of golf, or a calm conversation with your mate? Whatever you choose is a matter of preference. Consciously choosing and being straightforward about those choices is healthier for the relationship.

> Diego and Evelina faced a different problem. Diego's work as a civil engineer did not limit the places he could find employment as much as Evelina's profession as a sociologist did. She had specialized in Latin American relations and policy. After years of study, she completed her doctorate. The only career opportunities that appealed to her were in Washington, D.C.—thousands of miles away from Diego and Evelina's native Los Angeles.
>
> Diego had to make a decision he never envisioned himself facing; he might need to relocate so his wife could pursue her career. After much soul searching, discussion, and investigation, he decided he would support their move.
>
> Questions from their friends, family, and coworkers were awkward, but they knew their marriage was top priority. Diego and Evelina realized that a happy marriage is created between *two* happy people. Washington, D.C., would make Evelina happy, so that is where they moved.

WORK WITH—NOT
AGAINST—EACH OTHER

"I felt as if I ended up competing with my wife all the time," said Xavier, a lawyer. "I competed against her job, her friends, her latest cause. We would even compete about the kids. After awhile I decided I wasn't up for the competition, so I just started focusing on the children and my work. I really want a companion who will work with me, not against me. It's important to have that harmony and sense of spirit together. If not, the relationship becomes more work."

Xavier operated on the principle that the more energy and love he gave to others, the more he would receive in return. His wife, Angela, operated on the principle that everything had limits.

Many businesses are run on the same principle that Angela followed, and she ran her home like a corporation. She competed to earn or get her share of love and attention, and Xavier got caught up in the competition.

Commitment and love are not commodities. They are not enumerated or exchanged. They are *shared*. Exchanging fosters competition; sharing engenders harmony. It depends on which philosophy you adopt. Once you determine how you view relationships, you're free to compete within it or let the competition go and allow the relationship to thrive.

Creating the atmosphere in which two professionals can thrive in a relationship takes trust, confidence, and support. It also requires a lot of careful listening and acceptance. Don't forget to throw in some room to breathe.

After some counseling, Xavier and Angela decided to re-evaluate their priorities and adopt an "easy does it" attitude toward their marriage and careers. This change in attitude helped each remember to be patient and focus on what was most important to them—each other.

Today, Xavier feels more comfortable with Angela's career, and she's happy with their family. When one of them has little time or is very pressured, the other gently reminds them they're in it together. Then they can sort out demands on their time and decide again on their priorities. Both of them continue to choose—and get—what they really want.

THE CHALLENGE FOR MINORITIES

Because roles for men and women are more definitely prescribed among ethnic minorities, the challenge is to seek and maintain a balance between traditional and contemporary cultural values. On home and work fronts, ethnic minorities are forging a frontier, opening new career options, and developing new lifestyles in relationships. Dealing with family and friends, with expectations and changing cultural values, with the needs and desires of each other, and with the changes inherent in the development of any relationship are the ongoing demands made on ethnic minority, dual-career relationships today.

You must grant yourself permission to forge new ground. Determine what you want and need and clarify what you're willing to do to develop the kind of relationship and lifestyle you want. These steps will help you in your quest for personal satisfaction. Possible criticism from family and friends, the lack of role models who have met these challenges before, and the limited number of those doing so even now make the challenge—and the rewards—all the greater.

Chapter 18

Balancing Family &
Professional
Commitments

The balancing act of a professional who also has family responsibilities can be a difficult one. If you find yourself in this situation, you may feel guilty when you have to choose between a family function and a responsibility at work. You may not like to have to leave your loved ones when you must be away on business. You may even experience flashes of resentment when you have to put a job on hold so you can fulfill a family commitment or say "no" to family again because of professional responsibilities.

These problems can all weigh heavily on a professional with a burgeoning career. For women and ethnic minorities in particular, making decisions about these weighty questions is not always easy; nor are the alternatives clearly cut.

Every decision you make holds the potential for loss and a chance for growth. The ease with which you make a decision depends on how sure you are of your choices and how you perceive your decisions. There is only one of you, and only so much you can do. Only *you* can honestly tell what is most important to you, and *you* must live with your decision.

WHO DOES WHAT?

Depending on the partners in a relationship, "who does what?" is a common question, one that may be negotiated openly or work itself out over time. Two working professionals might end up sharing the responsibilities of cooking dinner, caring for the children or doing home repairs.

For some couples, the division of labor is automatic, especially if they both come from similar backgrounds and if they accept the roles traditionally prescribed. If one or both of the partners doesn't automatically have roles cast in her mind, or if they come from a traditional background but want to change who does what, some negotiation needs to take place.

Ethnic-minority couples often struggle with this issue because minority men *and* women frequently have fixed ideas of who should do what. When both people are working outside the home, the reality of what gets done versus what "should" get done and by whom is very different. If both are open and communicative, a couple can discuss their options, decide on a course of action, and make the transition. If one is rigid about who does what, negotiations can be much more difficult.

> Beulah took a position as an assistant district attorney right out of law school. Her husband, Washington, encouraged her to take the job. They failed to discuss how things would change and be handled at home. Beulah figured Wash would help her out with the cooking and child care or they could hire some help; it never crossed Wash's mind.

"It's your decision to work, " he told Beulah. "But don't forget the kids and the house, too."

"I can't, Wash," she responded. "I'm not a machine who can do everything. I need some help . . . I need your help!"

After some negotiating and much patience on her part, Beulah and Wash settled on hiring some help and splitting the chores. Some time later Washington reflected, "It sure is different from the way my Mom and Dad did things, but then my Mom and Dad weren't a couple of lawyers, either. I guess things are different, so we need to do things differently."

THE QUESTION OF CHILDREN

A common dilemma facing professional couples today is *if* and *when* they should start a family. The prime childbearing years coincide with the prime years for building a career; couples must decide and plan how to handle growing careers and a growing family simultaneously.

Those on a "fast track" tend to postpone having children until they are professionally established. But the biological clock ticks more loudly as the rewards of work add up. Sometimes couples wait to start their family until they take that extra cruise, receive another promotion, or buy a bigger home and car, only to find when they're ready that they have difficulty conceiving.

Ethnic-minority professionals often come from backgrounds where people start having families at an early age. The decision to have children is often influenced by a person's family expectations. The "right" time to start a family must be predicated on the couple's readiness (couples must realize there never will be a "perfect" time to start a family). In the meantime, handling pressures from the couple's families can be a challenge.

Rita was thirty-four and her husband, Juan, was thirty-seven. They had been busy building their careers, buying a house, investing, and traveling. When Rita was within ear-shot, her mother would repeatedly lament to friends, "Rita's out doing her thing, but she hasn't given me my grandchildren. I'll probably never be a nana." After several attempts at explaining their decision to wait to have children, Rita finally told her mother privately, "Mom, I love you and I love Juan and I love kids. We'll have a family, but when we're ready. You and I will have a great time when we do, OK?"

"Well, I guess OK," Rita's mother replied. "I was just worried." With that the issue was acknowledged and some limits were set. There was no need to be offensive. Let the overinvolved relative know you are aware of her concern and that you appreciate it. Reassure them things will go well.

RAISING CHILDREN

After the children come, life gets much more complicated. The board meeting has been scheduled for the same evening as the PTA meeting you promised to attend. You've made your reservations for the company's awards banquet—you've gone for years—but you learn it's the same night as the Little League game, and your little Jamie is pitching. Your service group is holding a fund raiser, but you also promised that this time you would help make the costumes for the school play.

As with any decision-making process, you must start by weighing your priorities. Try to get a little perspective on the situation. Ask yourself, "In the scheme of things, how important is the event? A month from now, who will remember my presence?" Get into the habit of distinguishing between a one-time-only event and a routine duty. Beyond wrestling with the ramifications of office politics, identify what is most important in the long run. Maybe a few quality hours with your child as she begins a new endeavor would do you both more good than your attending another cocktail party. On the other hand, sometimes children need to learn to wait while parents fulfill their work obligations.

> Christina exhausted herself trying to do it all. She was the high producer at work, an active community leader on advisory committees, a loving wife, and a frazzled mother. A typical day could include a trip from the airport to the grocery store, dropping her daughter off at ballet lessons on her way to her own aerobics class, and an appointment at the hairdresser before a banquet later that evening. She might attend an emergency meeting at the office late in the afternoon, then rush to change in time for the prebanquet VIP cocktail reception her boss had asked her to attend. Whew!

Understandably, Christina began to feel the grind. Tired most of the time, she grew resentful; before long, she started to feel as if she had failed. The more tired she grew, the less she could do and the more self-critical she became.

STOP THE CYCLE OF FRUSTRATION

Like so many of today's professionals, Christina didn't understand that, while it's true you can have it all, you can't necessarily have it all at the same time. There are a few realities over which you have no control. One is that children are only young once, while career opportunities may arise at various times.

You have to set your priorities and stick with them. Then you must absolve yourself of guilt. *No one* is everything to everybody all the time; you don't need to be either.

THE FAMILY'S OPINION

Familial interference is common among some families, but with ethnic minorities it poses an especially touchy problem.

Ethnic minorities usually come from a background where the family is very closely knit, but the professional has probably gone through several transitions or separations from family that have forced him or her to become more independent and less tied to the family nest. Other family members often have an idea of what the professional couple "should" be doing, and they may exert pressure.

> "I can't believe you guys are moving again," Charlene told her brother Carl. "I thought by now you would be done with school and all this career stuff and come back home and settle down. The folks are getting older, and we all miss you. How important is work, anyway? Don't we even matter any more?"
>
> "Of course you matter. Mom and Dad matter," Carl responded, sighing. "But there are things my wife and I need to do. We try to get to as many functions here with the family as possible, and I feel terrible when we miss out, but it's just not always possible, Charlene. If I'm not at the office making sure people are on top of things, the whole business starts to unravel. Shirley needs to continue school. I don't expect people to like all of our choices, but I hope you can be understanding."

That's about all you can do. Explain things to your family. Include them in your life when possible, and keep extending yourself to them. Keep them informed about the decisions you're making and the changes you are undergoing. If possible, have them visit your home and work place so they can better understand the pressures in your life.

Don't expect them to embrace your decisions fully. For lack of understanding, selfish reasons, or out of other concerns, family members will not always sound supportive. Be patient with them if you can, and keep them posted on what you're doing. They need to adjust to your routine just as you do. Because they're not around it the way you are, it will seem more foreign to them. You can explain things, but don't feel you must always justify your choices. Be consistent and communicative, then wait and see how things evolve.

Don't expect small children to understand your work pressures either. To satisfy their needs, try to set aside private time with them each day. Talk with them, read a book, go for a walk . . . do some kind of activity where you can interact, just you and your children. (Turn off the TV and video games.) Let the children know you have set aside time for them, then stick with it. If they can count on you to be there some time during each day, it might be easier for them to relax and take the pressure off you.

When older children complain about your schedule, take time to explain them as fully as you can without too much detail. Show the children where you work and describe the kinds of things you do. Keep a family schedule book where everyone can see what's coming up and what will be expected of them. Older children and teenagers can learn to respect your time—and their own.

Some years in child rearing are tougher than others, in the same way that some years in careers are tough, so take things a day at a time. Learn to ask for help. Be open and communicative with your children. Keep them informed of what is happening with you and with the family. Explain, explain, and explain again, then be patient. Change is painful, and it takes time to adjust.

PARTNERS—HOW MUCH TOGETHERNESS IS ENOUGH?

Another dilemma facing professional couples is that of finding enough time with their mate to maintain a healthy, affectionate relationship. Because the relationship between two adults is different from the relationship between an adult and a child, the dynamics, needs, rewards, and consequences are also different. It becomes a question of balance.

"It's so upsetting," Wanda lamented. "Every time I want to do something, go to lunch with my friends, do volunteer work, or even go to church, Albert complains. He says I'm not spending enough time with him. Granted, I'm busy much of the time, but I do spend time with him. Besides, I need other people and different activities. I go ahead most of the time and do what I want to do, but he drags me down or punishes me by sulking or complaining when I return home."

Deciding what is the right amount of time together is the key to handling a partner who discourages and dampens your brightest plans. Start by looking at your assumptions. People often believe that because they are in a relationship with someone, they should spend all their free time together, enjoy the same activities, and have the same friends. Be honest. Maybe you really don't care that much about spark plugs, or you find pottery boring. Perhaps even your partner's friends are a bit hard to take. It's possible for each of you to retain your individuality and still function together as a couple.

Before you dismiss someone's complaint that you're not around enough, review your schedule and see if it's true. Maybe you're too busy because extra demands have been placed on you. Maybe you've somehow made yourself unavailable to avoid dealing with a troubled relationship. You may not be around enough, but there must be a reason why.

Control is often the real issue. Some people need to feel as if they are always in charge, so they try to dictate who should go where, and with whom, and when. If you don't check things out with them, they will try to make you check in. You might be involved in a struggle to see "who's boss."

Some people need more attention than others. If you're involved with someone who can't seem to get enough of your time, you may still hear complaints even after you really cut down on outside activities.

Occasionally one person decides that the other is "all I want." The "chosen one" will be expected to become lover, parent, confidante, mentor, financial advisor, sibling, and best friend. This kind of relationship is a trap. When it finally disintegrates, and it usually does, it leaves one person feeling drained and the other cheated.

In some cases, revenge may also be operating. If you insist he do something, he might insist on something from you, such as staying home.

Then there's helplessness. You may worry that the other person won't survive if you're not around, at least not happily. The truth is, the only difference your staying will make is that the other person will be unhappy in your presence! If that person's happiness depends on your activities, you'll always hear complaints or heavy sighs. Each of us has to accept responsibility for our own happiness. It is no one else's obligation.

One way to counter the objections of clinging partners is to offer them choices. You won't be together all the time, but you will be there a limited number of times that are most important to them. Keeping your priorities in mind, try to arrive at a compromise, then stick with it.

THE FOLKS BACK HOME

Of the many stresses and losses you face, watching your own parents grow older is one of the toughest. Maybe it's difficult because the timing between parents and children falls out of synchronization ever so slightly with each passing year. When you reach the point of making peace with yourself and with them, they are that much further along in their own lives and have passed the point in adulthood that you're now ready to share with them.

Now that you finally appreciate the skills it takes to deal with career pressures, your folks are retired. You're raising children, while their child-rearing days are over. As you struggle to build a financial nest egg, they are adjusting to living off theirs. Just as you're winding up, they start winding down.

The slowing down can be a big adjustment, especially if your parents have been very active. The challenge is subtly and delicately to wrestle responsibilities away from them, while making sure their pride and yours are left intact. Then comes the tug-of-war between your responsibility to your parents and your responsibility to your own needs. Nagging doubts and personal reservations hound you. Slowly you switch roles, responsibilities, and ways of approaching things.

Just as parents sometimes think of their adult offspring as if they were still children, children often retain old views of their parents. Grown children often keep an image of their parents as strong and in charge, able to do more and to do it better and faster. Sometimes it comes as a shock when these adult children realize that this is no longer so.

The truth is that your parents never did know it all; nor could they ever do it all. You were simply a child who thought they could. Now that you're grown, you must face their limitations.

Moreover, like everyone else, the needs and interests of parents change as they grow older. Maybe they don't care to do as much and as quickly as they did before. Former activities may no longer interest them. They may be reluctant to take on as much responsibility as they used to.

Finally, just because you may be able to accept the changes that come with aging doesn't mean your parents will. Sometimes they can't acknowledge, much less accept, their limitations or losses. They might refuse to help or deny they are tired. For a while denial works, but only for a while. Eventually, adjustments must be made.

Look for signs that your parents are slowing down and anticipate the changes. Don't expect or plan as much. Leave a margin for time and error. Sometimes things take longer and people make mistakes, so work on your patience.

174

There are services in the community for aging parents. Whether it's to help them build new friendships, stabilize health problems, combat depression, or work with their memory, these services can help relieve the burden of family members who aren't sure what to do.

Parents and children are often like ships that pass in the night—they give signals but often miss each other. Roles are reversing, and that means stress and loss. Give yourself time to grieve. Listen to them more. Ask questions and talk with, not at, them. If you can, forgive any grudges you still hold against them. Despite their imperfections (and yours), be grateful for whatever they have done and whatever you have learned as a result.

Chapter 19

Dealing with Stress
in Your Life

Essential to fine performance is keeping yourself in good shape mentally, physically, and spiritually. Minority professionals face the same challenges as others professionals, and then some. This chapter focuses on stress; its signs and symptoms, and some solutions. It outlines the essentials to taking good care of yourself.

DEFINING STRESS

Stress is your body's readiness to respond to its environment. A baby's cry, the phone awakening you from your sleep, extreme weather, work deadlines, and other stimuli cause your heart to beat faster, your palms to sweat or become cold, your pupils to dilate and your muscles to feel increased tension.

The adrenaline pumped through your body allows you to face the challenge or run from it.

If you have too many demands placed on you, adrenaline is pumped into your system continuously, as if a faucet has been left running. Your heart will beat faster and your mind might race almost continuously, or you could suffer fatigue, irritability, insomnia, or other symptoms.

Everyone has his or her own "setpoint," or amount of stress that is optimum for functioning. That's the point at which stress provides enough stimuli to keep you motivated but not so much that you're overwhelmed. Stress serves as a source of energy to "keep you going." The only time you won't experience any stress is when you're dead; the lowest amount experienced is usually when you're asleep. If you watch your body's reactions to stress, you can plan for it and regulate it accordingly.

Some minority professionals seem to thrive on stress, while others find it hard to cope with. The combination of goals, education, finances, work or academic status, support system, and family demands can cause excessive levels of stress for the minority professional who is trying to cover too much ground. The conflict between two sets of cultural values (see chapter 4, page 39) leaves that professional walking the tightrope between two systems but never comfortably fitting in either one.

SYMPTOMS OF STRESS

Your body tells you how well you're handling stress in your life. Headaches, backaches, ulcers, colitis, diarrhea or constipation, indigestion, sleep problems, overeating or lack of appetite, increased drinking, smoking, or other use of substances to "feel better," tension, skin rashes, hair loss, bouts of crying, poor concentration, outbursts of anger, and heart attacks—these are some of the most common physical signs of stress.

Many people don't pay close enough attention to their bodies to catch the subtle changes that occur early in a stress reaction. Instead, they'll "let things go" and suddenly end up sick or unable to function well. Watch your body for signs of the wear and tear of stress on your system. The earlier you perceive stress, the better your chances of controlling it.

CAUSES OF STRESS

There are two major categories of stressors—external and internal. *External stressors* are conditions or events that occur around you but are not necessarily caused by you. *Internal stressors* stem from how you think. While not all stressors can be controlled, your response to them is your choice.

External Stressors

Severe hot or cold weather, windowless offices lit only by fluorescent lights, equipment that doesn't quite "fit" you, holidays, promotions or firings, your salary, your relatives coming for a visit and staying . . . and staying . . . and staying . . . These things are not always under your complete control, but they do cause stress. To some extent you can choose which aspects you manage and how you respond overall. But minorities face more than their fair share. Underemployment, family struggles, and the demands of others for financial assistance can stretch a minority professional's stamina beyond the point usually experienced by non-minority professionals.

Critical life events or "passages" in life are in another category of external stressors. Separation, divorce, remarriage, pregnancy, childbirth, children's transitions through school, coping with aging parents, and death and dying are significant events that happen to most people in the course of living. Adjustment to the changes is fairly predictable; each one entails grief and loss. Shock or denial, anger or disappointment, depression and anxiety, resolution or acceptance and feelings of hope all accompany these changes if the grief and loss are handled successfully. Each loss is accompanied by a gain, but the key is to allow the former and receive the latter. Then you can move on to the next challenge.

Internal Stressors

Internal stressors occur between your ears—they have to do with how you think and react. You can't always control external stressors that happen about you, but you can choose to control your internal stressors—how you respond to them.

Beliefs are your way of thinking, and they are the foundation of how you think and act. Irrational beliefs appear to be true, but they have a twist of illogic that causes stress.

> Anabelle believed, "It's up to me to make my relationship work." It seemed to her that a dedicated wife should believe that. Anabelle tried to follow her belief, although her husband was an alcoholic. For years she struggled with his denial, lies, unfulfilled dreams, and broken promises. She tried being a "better" wife, caring for the children, keeping an immaculate house, and preparing his favorite meals, but to no avail. He still drank.
>
> After some professional help, a lot of support, and some serious soul searching, she realized that two people must be involved in making a marriage a success. Her partner wasn't holding up his end of the deal.

Other irrational beliefs entail people-pleasing statements, such as, "People must be happy; I must make them happy." Happiness is an inside job. If someone's unhappy, you can't fix it. Only the unhappy person can.

Work-horse statements, such as, "If I don't do it, no one will" can help you feel indispensable. But they can also make you feel very tired.

The martyrlike belief that "The more I do for them, the more they'll appreciate me" feeds a big case of resentment in you and provides fuel if you use guilt as a weapon against others. While the martyr might have a self-righteous sense of being better than everyone else, this belief seldom gets much more than resistance and heavy sighs from others.

Irrational beliefs faced by minority professionals are discussed elsewhere in this book. Being betrayed by your own and being "the only" are covered in chapter 10, page 89. Taking risks is dealt with in chapter 13, page 119, and how you relate to others is discussed in chapter 16, page 149. These situations and problems often dictate how much stress you can handle effectively.

Check your belief system. If you keep running in circles or are frustrated by doing things that don't yield the benefits you want, perhaps you have some type of irrational belief operating. Once you discover that, you can change how you think and how you feel.

Morris Massey, a professor at the University of Colorado, has written that a person's values are heavily influenced by whatever was occurring socially in the world around the time the person was ten years old. People who were raised in the Depression are typically "thrifty," watching how and what they buy. They often question banking practices, are cautious when using credit (if they use it at all), and have conservative political opinions. They also save—foil, string, plastic bags, old clothing . . . things that can be used and often things that can't.

Children who grew up in the 1960s have a very different orientation. Their youth was filled with "sex, drugs, and rock and roll," the Vietnam conflict, "flower children," or hippies, and a burgeoning awareness of civil rights. As adults, they often question authority, are independent thinkers, and support the rights of others to "do their thing."

Those raised with technology in the 1970s and 1980s believe very differently. They are accustomed to having their information, their problems, even their food, processed very rapidly. To wait for a college degree or a career to blossom often seems like an eternity. Impatience, an increased need for information (but not necessarily the wisdom to go with it), and an incessant craving for more typify this group.

When a working veteran of World War II, with his conservative work-ethic beliefs of common good, encounters a high-tech baby with a drive to make it big, and quick, you've got a clash of ideas and values. You've also got stress.

If you're in an uncomfortable situation, ask whether a clash of values is occurring. While you can't change someone else's way of thinking, you can better understand and accommodate it and reduce your stress.

Cultural values and the stress they can produce are discussed in chapter 4 "Understanding Cultural Diversity" (see page 39). If one set of values under which you operate conflicts with another, you'll feel it.

Ramona managed her office like clockwork. Organized and "in charge," she gathered information, assigned tasks, and balanced the budget skillfully. She had the competitive edge over others and had mastered what it took to get ahead. But when she returned home every evening to her family, it was a different story. Her husband expected the house to be in perfect order, the children to be well-behaved, and dinner to be ready. But he didn't want Ramona to be too forceful in getting things that way. When she began to delegate duties, discipline the children, or ask for his help, he often responded, "Hey, Ramona, you're not at work, you know! You might need help handling things, but you don't need to order us around."

"Order him around!" she thought to herself. "All I did was ask directly. He's just not used to having someone else in charge." She mentally began to make the shift back into the traditional cultural system developed across the years, leaving for a while the competitive one that had helped her accomplish so much at work.

The shift from cooperation to competition, modesty to speaking up, from primarily considering others in making decisions to deciding what is good based on individual needs, can cause confusion and conflict. The more delicate and dynamic the balancing act between value systems, the greater the stress you'll feel.

Take a good look at expectations—yours and those of others. If you have one idea of how things should be and they have another, you'll experience stress. Ask what people want and what they expect. Make your needs and expectations known. Inform people what you are willing and able to do. If you can, come to some kind of understanding so you can proceed with minimal confusion. The more closely your expectations are aligned, the less stress you'll feel.

FIVE QUESTIONS TO HELP IDENTIFY STRESS

There are five steps you can take to help reduce your level of stress. You need to ask yourself the following five questions. Once you've answered them, you'll have a better idea of how to deal with the stress you're experiencing.

What Are the Symptoms?

You feel anxious, your stomach or back aches, that rash is getting worse and so is your irritability, your patience is wearing thin, and your concentration is equally poor—these are some common signs of stress. Pay close attention to ongoing situations so that things don't suddenly overwhelm you.

What's Happening?

If the guy at the next desk in your office is cracking his chewing gum day and night, if your supervisor is unduly criticizing you or if the company's budget just went down the tubes, you need to understand the dynamics of the situation to assess your options. Put your finger on what's happening; then you can begin to zero in on a solution.

What Needs to Change?

Many things might need changing—maybe the payroll system at work, maybe your spouse's spending habits, maybe your attitudes toward life. Be honest. Don't take any shortcuts, and no buck passing, either.

Who Needs to Change It?

If the answer is anybody except you, good luck. Other people, places, and events are beyond your control, so don't fall into the trap of fixing anything except *yourself*.

What's the Plan?

If you can't change everything around you, you can at least choose how you respond. That's the most important aspect of the problem, and it's about all that ultimately matters.

The key word in solving these and other problems is *choice*. You may not like your options, but you always have a choice about which ones you choose to exercise. Even deciding *not* to decide is a decision. Become aware of your choices, weigh the consequences, and choose as wisely as you can. Then feel your stress decrease.

Ways to Help Relieve Stress

The five techniques described below can help you a great deal. They are ways of rethinking a situation or giving your thoughts a "tune-up" to help you reduce your stress level.

Reframing

Pretend you're watching a video of a stressful situation in which you're involved. In your mind, press the "pause" button. Examine what is *really* happening in the situation. Decipher what your role and responsibilities are, then take charge of them. Let go of whatever is not yours.

If your boss comes in and suddenly blasts you with a barrage of criticism, ask yourself whether there is any merit to what he says. If you blew it, accept the responsibility and fix it. If the criticism is unfounded, you can see it for what it is and try to understand why it's happening. Maybe his bosses are putting pressure on him. Maybe his health is failing or he's struggling with a personal problem. Maybe it's the only way he knows to relate to other people.

If you're frustrated with another person's prejudice or you've experienced discrimination, look at the situation from a different angle. In addition to insulting you, the person who treats you unfairly also undermines his or her own credibility on the job. You weren't the only one humiliated; the perpetrator was also humiliated.

Try to see the "up" side of the situation. A loss or disappointment may actually open the way to a better opportunity. A negative situation may teach an important lesson, if you're tuned into it. Any loss ultimately results in growth, if you're willing to work through it. Look at the opportunity instead of the danger, and feel your stress decrease.

Imagination

A sense of humor will carry you far. The ability to laugh with, not at, someone is an important key to enjoying your work while building positive relationships with your colleagues. If you've ever worked for someone who takes everything seriously, you know that humor can add a new perspective to a difficult situation. Try to see the human foibles, the idiosyncracies, the odd contradictions in situations, and they won't seem so overwhelming.

> In the office where Irene worked as a secretary, the photocopier jammed after every 15 copies. To remedy the situation, Irene had to lower the front lid, stick her hand between the two copier drums to release the entangled paper then begin again. Her hand was always blackened by toner when she loosened the jammed wad.
>
> One day Marissa came in to the copy room to give Irene some documents to copy. There was Irene, on her knees in front of the machine, hands clasped as she peered woefully inside. As Marissa approached, Irene glanced up and gave her a "Don't-you-dare-ask-me-to-make-copies-for-you!" look.
>
> Marissa stopped a moment and assessed the situation. "Irene, I don't think praying to the machine will make it work any better!" she said. The tension broken, both handled their irritability and the situation with a different perspective.

Minorities are often noted for maintaining a sense of humor, despite the odds they face. Whether through joking, singing, or some other diversion, minorities have historically relied on humor to survive.

As a minority professional, you'll need your sense of humor often. Dull meetings, routine tasks, and coworkers or supervisors who take everything seriously, and daily struggles for getting ahead can be combatted with a light touch.

Whispering

"Whispering" is the ability to send yourself positive messages. If you don't do it, others probably won't either. Tell yourself that you're valuable, that you've done a good job, and that you're worthy of good things happening to you. On the days when you get no encouragement or gratitude from others, give it to yourself. After all, who knows you better and who deserves it more?

Minority professionals need to develop and hone their whispering skills. The pressures of someone scrutinizing your work, of being a pioneer or "the only" in a work situation, and working as hard or harder than others for less pay and recognition can result in negative self-talk and lowered self-esteem. Whispering helps keep confidence and energy levels up.

Faith

Whether based in a formal religion or your own belief that life has a master plan, faith assures you that things work out for the best in a typically orderly, reasonable way. This skill can be crucial, especially if you have the tendency to want to control things. Faith gives you the day off from control—permanently.

It is this faith, not the situation itself, that requires constant work and attention. Develop that, and the stress of having to take care of everything will ease.

Surrendering

Understanding what you *can* control and accepting those things you *can't* allows you to let go of those preoccupations and concerns that cause stress. The sooner you choose not to wrestle with a problem or let your life be run by it, the sooner you can turn it over to a Higher Power. You can then start living as you were intended.

If you believe you've let go of a problem, but it still bothers you, you haven't completely surrendered. For high-achieving professionals, especially minorities, surrender-ing—giving up control—can be the toughest skill to master.

If you look more closely, you'll notice that things are out of your control anyway. You might as well delegate your worry and surrender in peace.

MAINTAINING BALANCE IN YOUR LIFE

Six components are essential to maintain "balance" in your life so that you can take care of yourself. They are not listed in order of priority, but each should be practiced regularly.

Work

Work absorbs the largest part of your day for the majority of your adult years, so it is probably the easiest to figure into your plan of self-care. Your time on the job provides structure, challenge, meaning, and friendships. When people retire, they often miss these unspoken benefits of work that kept a healthy balance in their daily lives for many years.

It's easy for work to consume an inordinate amount of a professional's time, especially if you're trying to establish yourself and are being rewarded for your efforts. Weekend time might be harder to structure because of the absence of work, though professionals often choose to work on weekends, too. Watch carefully how and when you spend your work time. Of all aspects of life that can take over a professional's life, work will do it. You must decide whether you will allow that to happen.

For minorities trying to "make it big" professionally, an emphasis on the technical aspects of work—its quality and quantity—can be strong. Overwork, with marginal returns, is an easy trap to fall into. It's one you want to avoid.

Rest

Rest does not mean simply sleep (most professionals never get enough). It is the time you allow yourself to be in "neutral gear," easing up enough to renew your spirit and regain the energy to continue all your other duties.

Rest is crucial for professionals, because without it creativity is stifled. If you're having difficulty solving problems or coming up with new approaches to work, try resting more.

Exercise

Many people claim they don't have the energy to exercise. Chances are they don't have the energy because they don't exercise. A twenty-minute session at least three times a week will get your heart moving and clear your mind.

Start with something you might enjoy that fits well into your schedule. Give yourself six weeks to form a new exercise habit. After that, you'll miss it if you step out of routine.

Play

Not so deep inside of everyone is a child who's ready to play and have fun. Don't ignore that child too long. If you feel over-stressed, tired, or deprived, ask yourself whether you've been spending enough time playing. Chances are you haven't.

Many professionals grow up learning to be "productive" with their time, so they don't always know how to cut loose and simply play. If you have difficulty playing, find someone who doesn't, then let them teach you how. It will release a source of creativity and energy in you and free you from the daily grind of responsibility.

Nutrition

Refined sugar, white flour, caffeine, alcohol, drugs, salt, and fat don't do people much good. The foods you consume fuel your daily activities and your ability to think clearly.

Minorities may suffer more from nutrition-based problems, such as diabetes and hypertension. Obesity and its complications, malnutrition, and lowered school or work performance accompany poor nutrition. Minority professionals do not necessarily suffer malnutrition or other food problems, but years of poor eating habits and genetic predisposition can significantly increase the risks.

Volumes have been written about the importance of good nutrition. Find a basic nutrition book and follow its guidelines. There aren't any easy shortcuts with nutrition. Discipline yourself about good eating habits the same way you discipline your work routine. It will pay great dividends in the amount of energy you have, how you feel, and your overall outlook on life.

Spirituality

Spirituality is the aspect most professionals need most but have developed the least. Whether based in a formal religion or cultivated as a sense of a Higher Power that keeps the order of life intact, spirituality is crucial to maintaining a balanced outlook that is not self-centered.

Carl Jung has stated that the only substantial change an adult can make is a spiritual one. For most professionals, another cruise, one more promotion, an additional project, a fancier car, more clothes, greater prestige, membership in certain organizations, or becoming involved with certain people just don't fill that void, that longing, that wanting "something more" that will make a difference.

Put your spiritual life at the top of your list. If you do, everything else will fall into place more easily.

Chapter 20

Happy or Hooked?
Handling
Addictions

What begins innocently as an extra drink over happy hour, a casual sexual fling that doesn't "mean anything," an extra, unnecessary purchase, or another serving of food when you're full can be the beginning of a nightmare—addiction.

Minority professionals by nature are often driven, compulsive, and perfectionistic; these traits are all central to addiction. Work, family and financial pressures, fatigue, anger, loneliness or other unexpressed feelings, and possibly a biological predisposition to developing addictive problems make professionals prime targets for "getting hooked."

UNDERSTANDING THE POWER
OF ADDICTION

If you've ever wished for a "quick fix" from stress, you're not alone. When pressures at work begin to mount and hassles at home start to build, or when your routine becomes a rut, the "great escape" looks extremely appealing.

Some people try a nap; others try a weekend away. Sometimes burying your nose in a book helps, or even just daydreaming the dullness away.

More often, though, these remedies aren't enough, and people look for more relief. They grab a candy bar, take a pill, smoke a cigarette, drink a few extra scotch and waters, blow a wad of cash, work a little harder, do some extra exercises, or have an affair—just for a little diversion.

It sounds innocent enough, but before you know it, it's out of control. You have to eat the whole bag of chips, not just a serving. Food becomes more than nutrition; it's an obsession. Soon, it takes more pot, more pills, more cocaine to do the trick. You go from a few cigarettes to a pack or more a day. The drinks have increasingly more scotch than water. Money spent during wild shopping sprees soon exceeds your income. Your exercise habits become exhaustive. One unsatisfying love affair leads to another, leaving behind a string of victims.

Whatever the addiction, the phenomenon is the same. It's a disease. It is *chronic* (it won't go away, but it's treatable), *progressive* (it worsens with time) and *fatal* (it kills, one way or another, if left untreated). While most people would argue that everyone has a vice or two, not many would admit that their vice is getting out of hand. You need to know if you're hooked.

SIGNS OF ADDICTION

Addicts have one main goal—to use whatever they are hooked on to get relief. The euphoria of cocaine, the slow numbing of alcohol, the "mellow mood" of marijuana, the thrill of gambling or another sexual affair, the brief feeling of power in spending, the calm after smoking and the sedative or energizing effect of food help a person escape discomfort or pain. An addiction takes hold because it takes greater amounts of the substance or activity to get the same effect over time. Before you know it, you're hooked.

Other aspects of life take a back seat to this goal. Responsibilities at work, at home, to friends, and to the community become less important. The addict begins to care as little about others as he does about himself. Sexual relationships and general health begin to deteriorate.

People who are hooked usually know they have a problem, but denial is a big part of the disease, so they lie about it to themselves and to others.

"I don't really eat that much; I just have a slow metabolism," says the overeater.

"I'll only gamble until I break even. Then I'll quit," is the common refrain of the gambler.

"So what if there have been lots of women. They're all one-night stands. No big deal. They didn't mean anything to me anyway," argues the sex addict.

But it *does* matter, and the addict knows it. For the person addicted to spending money, his out-of-control habit can be terrifying, especially when the bills roll in. Smoking matters to the addict when she can't catch her breath. Working compulsively stops paying off when you lose your family and friends because you're "married" to your job.

To cover up, the addict becomes secretive—eating, drinking, smoking, spending, or carousing quietly behind the scenes—while trying to maintain a respectable facade for outsiders. The one who's hooked makes promises he won't keep. He can be charming and manipulative, saying or doing whatever it takes to get his way. When he fails, the addict blames others for his mistakes or shortcomings. He always looks outward because it's too terrifying to look inward. He fears what he'll find, but when he does finally peer inside, he discovers what everyone else has known all along; he's hooked.

General health usually deteriorates with addiction. The addict can experience extreme weight loss or weight gain, anxiety, insomnia, mood swings, blackouts, absent-mindedness, and injury. As the disease progresses, some or all of these afflictions can appear.

Family and friends suffer as much as the addict. In the family with an alcoholic mother, the children become increasingly afraid and react by taking over the responsibilities or withdrawing.

At work, coworkers soon tire of the addict's lies and refuse to help him cover up the problem. Spouses become frantic with worry, trying hard to control what is beyond anyone's reach. That's why the disease is progressive. Just as it seems to get under control, it eludes the grasp of the addict and his or her loved ones.

Without treatment, the addiction will worsen and, ultimately, can kill the addict. Smokers live with the specter of lung cancer and other fatal respiratory diseases. People with eating disorders and those who compulsively overexercise flirt dangerously with heart attacks. Desperate gamblers venture into the underworld of loan sharks and criminals to borrow money for their unpaid gambling debts, not realizing that they could end up paying for those loans with their lives. Alcoholics face a slow death from cirrhosis of the liver or a quick ending at the wheel of an automobile while driving drunk. In today's world, substance abuse or promiscuity could mean contracting AIDS.

It may sound overly dramatic, but the reality is that an addiction is a slow, sure, self-inflicted death. In other words, it's suicide.

IT'S EASY TO GET HOOKED

Addictions thrive in every kind of environment. They are found among many different types of people—those who work and those who don't, those who are well-educated and school dropouts, CEOs and mailroom clerks, Blacks, Whites, Hispanics, Native Americans, and Asians.

Minorities in general suffer from drug and alcohol abuse at higher rates than non-minorities. Cocaine, alcohol, and work are common addictions of minority professionals.

Statistics indicate that if any kind of addiction runs in your family, your chances of being at risk are greatly increased. If you develop one kind of addiction, chances are you can develop others, too.

ADDICTIONS ARE DIFFICULT TO BREAK

When a person uses an addictive substance or participates in an addictive activity, his body responds euphorically, even if only for a moment. The flush of heightened sexual excitement, the release of endorphins into the system while exercising, the rush of adrenaline while beating the odds gambling, the pleasure of food, and the buzz from alcohol or from too much caffeine all kick in a pleasant—though fleeting—feeling.

Once a person "crashes" (comes out of the euphoric state back into reality), he seeks another high, so he pursues his activity more vigorously. If he isn't satisfied, he becomes anxious and desperately seeks relief, thus continuing the addictive cycle.

In its early stages, an addiction seduces its victims with many rewards. Workaholics get recognition, promotions, and pay raises. Gamblers win—at least sometimes. People with eating disorders feel a little better right after eating and sometimes win in the battle of the bulge. Sex addicts get lots of attention, positive and negative. Those who drink feel mellow and sexy; those who use drugs feel euphoric and powerful. Addicts won't be willing to give up these early rewards until they start to lose control and begin to give up on themselves.

THERE *IS* A WAY OUT

There's a way out, but first the problem must be acknowledged. Even if an addict doesn't seem to want help, the family and other loved ones can work together with a professional at a treatment center to conduct a loving confrontation called *intervention*. Most in-patient treatment centers conduct them for little or no charge. They are usually successful in getting the person into treatment.

In-patient care is often the best choice for someone who needs to be detoxified and stabilized before facing the world without "using." Treatment at an in-patient facility is followed by outpatient after-care to help ensure that the person does not relapse.

Sometimes addicts go "cold turkey" or seek exclusive individual counseling to break their habit. However, because part of the disease of addiction is isolation (the abuser feels "different" from other people), treatment in isolation often doesn't work well.

Group therapy can be a good alternative, but only if the addict stays "clean," sober or abstinent, and if he attends sessions regularly. Physicians sometimes prescribe drugs to treat addictions, but typically it is not advised: substances are the initial problem, and people can switch addictions from one substance to another.

The greatest travesty against addicts is the get-over-it-quick, no-pain "treatment" schemes. It doesn't matter if you drink premixed low-calorie milkshakes. If your compulsion to overeat is still raging, you'll gain the lost weight back, and probably more. Smokeless cigarettes promote denial. Harmless sexual interludes are non-existent, because at least one person (the addict) is overcome with guilt and shame.

Minority professionals often battle their addictions in silence. Pressured by performance demands, often lacking role models or confidantes on the job, and feeling isolated from friends and family, their addictions steadily worsen. Adding to their unhappiness, minority professionals who suffer addictions may be told, "We knew you couldn't handle the pressure (or the success)."

Generalizations about minorities are then often made.

- Latinos are Romeos.

- Blacks do drugs.

- Native Americans are alcoholics.

- Minorities just waste their success on bad habits.

The shame, guilt, and fear they feel from being hooked mounts as the addiction takes firm hold.

There are no quick cures! Face it—eating too much makes you fat, drinking to excess make you drunk, gambling and spending beyond your means wreaks financial havoc, smoking kills your lungs, drugs wipe out your body, and overwork destroys a balanced life.

Most addicts are intelligent, loving people who found a substance or activity to quell some deep-seated sadness or longing, to anesthetize emotional pain, or to avoid both closeness and being alone. This "shortcut" of handling discomfort costs dearly in the long run.

As mentioned earlier, a spiritual deficit is often at the bottom of an addiction, so its solution is usually a spiritual one. The 12-Step Self-Help Group Programs have been the most effective in helping people kick addictions.

Alcoholics Anonymous, Overeaters Anonymous, Narcotics Anonymous, Sex Addicts Anonymous, and other "Anonymous" groups are based on a spiritual program of recovery. Not affiliated with a religious denomination, these programs help the recovering person rediscover strength and hope through a Higher Power, whether within themselves, through God, or through others.

The addict will find in the twelve steps of the program a blueprint for living. If followed, the steps remove the compulsion for the addictive substance or activity. The program effectively allows the addict to admit powerlessness over the addiction, then receive help from their Higher Power to clear up the wreckage of the past in their lives and to develop a respectful, loving relationship with themselves, their Higher Power, and others.

A twelve-step program removes self-abuse as an option and replaces it with restored dignity and self-care. It shows that the individual pain is inevitable but that suffering is optional. It promotes progress, not perfection. It also shows how, day by day, the strength you need to go on with your life is at hand, if only you are willing to receive it.

If you or someone you love has an addiction problem, help is only a phone call away. Contact a mental health center, an addiction treatment facility, an addiction specialist, or any of the twelve-step programs for assistance.

The hardest part of stopping self-abuse is taking that first step. Do it now. You're worth it.

Chapter 21

Enjoying Your Rewards

People often talk about and work very hard for what they want—success—but deep down they're not fully convinced they deserve it. As a result, when the rewards roll in, they're unable to enjoy them or they aren't satisfied with what they're receiving.

For minorities, success and rewards tend to be a double-edged sword. On the one hand, you're told that competing, excelling, and making a contribution will "put you on the map." On the other hand, once you're on the map, you often find you're there alone. The mandates for success and the realities of success it brings must be reckoned with if a minority professional wants to advance in his or her career.

UNABLE TO ENJOY REWARDS

Theresa had always been told she should work hard for a living and "earn her keep." Every evening when she was a child her mother reviewed Theresa's day with her, pointing out her achievements and teaching her to be grateful for the good things in her life. Each achievement was recognized but not celebrated, so Theresa figured she wasn't doing enough somehow, or that her achievements had to be topped by yet another triumph, not relished for the moment.

In another scenario, picture Ricky as he walked jubilantly into the professor's office, his master's thesis in hand.

"I finished," he declared, smiling. "Corrections and all!"

"Great!" the professor responded. "Now, when are you going to start on your doctoral research?"

Deflated, Ricky later became angry. "It's the same old thing," he thought to himself. "When I was a kid my dad was never satisfied with what I did. If I got an A- he'd ask me why it wasn't an A. It seems as if nothing is ever enough."

Some people experience a different kind of cultural bind. Cecilia finally took the big step. She had saved enough money, enrolled at the university, and eventually completed her degree. Back home there was no celebration.

"Well, how's the college grad?" asked her sister a few days later, a sarcastic edge in her voice. "I don't imagine you want to join us for a movie, do you? I mean we don't have all that much that's interesting to talk about, and you might be bored."

A few days later, Cecilia received more of the same from her father but with a different slant.

"Cecilia, I know you think you're educated and all now. But you're still a member of this family and my daughter, and I don't want you to think you're better than all of us, understand?"

She simply nodded. But to herself she thought, "Understand? Sure. I understand what he's saying. Don't be too happy, don't get too confident, don't be too proud. They don't have a clue what this degree means to me and what the experience has been. All I know is that the last thing they're going to do with me is celebrate."

So goes the mandate.

Don't forget where you came from. Don't forget who you are. Don't change. With every "don't" there's another message: don't enjoy, either.

Very often, parents encourage their children to do well in school and at work. They are impressed at the thought that their child might earn more, have a better position than they did, own a boat or other "toys," go on vacations, have a nicer home, and accumulate plenty of possessions that show they are doing well. But they don't always encourage their children to be happier than they were. Some adult children work very hard to accomplish their goals and attain these things. But they don't allow themselves to enjoy their rewards, to be happier than other family members, especially their parents.

As a result, they get on the merry-go-round of work-buy-accumulate-work-buy-accumulate. But they don't really relish their success.

In some cases, minority professionals hold themselves back from enjoying their rewards because it somehow means they've "broken the mold," left everyone else behind, and chosen to be different. The loss of the camaraderie and standing in their own cultural group is great. They continue to work hard and achieve, but they don't enjoy their rewards.

If you're bound by mandates that keep you from delighting in your success, look at your sense of entitlement. It's the humble but sincere self-statement that says you deserve good things. Add to that another clause, "I also deserve to enjoy them."

Other people's concerns, mandates, or restrictive comments come out of resentment, envy, jealousy, or fear. They may see that you've done what perhaps they haven't. They see the future that awaits you and want it but haven't yet paid the price to earn it. Or they're afraid you'll change and leave them exactly where they are.

Not enjoying the fruits of your labor won't make others feel any more ambitious, secure, or happy. It will only keep you unfulfilled and frustrated. Enjoying your rewards won't make you any less "ethnic" or "feminine" or anything else that keeps you a member of the group. If anything, enjoying your success will encourage you to achieve more, broaden your horizons, and bring more to the group than you would have before. Losing part of the old group—that old mandate—is part of maturing, developing, and becoming wiser, even if it feels painful and disappointing.

Give yourself permission to enjoy. You deserve it, and you've earned it.

When "Things" Aren't Enough

The great "I want" seems to be a national epidemic. It's that gnawing condition of always wanting something, then not being satisfied once you've gotten it.

People want high-performance cars, stylish clothes, prestigious positions at work, the latest in electronic equipment, plus "a relationship." They believe they need these things to feel better, more complete, more secure. But problems arise when you get what you want and something *still* doesn't seem right.

> Mike was a slave to ambition. Up early and in bed late, his days were filled with project information, financial forecasts and briefings with his staff. Mike didn't have a simple business plan; he charted out his entire life for the next fifteen years in six-month segments. Achievement after achievement, position after position—the string of successes grew as he searched out yet another challenge.

"I love starting projects," Mike told a colleague. "Joint ventures, real estate development, you name it. I love going after it, getting it going, then moving on to another. It's so much fun just to go through the process over and over in so many different ways."

— — —

Betty had another process going—her "Search for the Perfect Mate." She thought she knew what she wanted, but she never seemed to get it. "I want someone who will be there for me and love me," Betty told a friend. "Someone who wants to build a life with me, who's interesting and active."

Instead of selecting potential partners with those attributes, Betty became involved with "The Impossibles": those unable to commit, the users and abusers, the neglectful, and some who simply didn't care. "I get fairly far with some who show an interest, but none of them ever turns into a long-term relationship. When I do meet someone who's eligible, appropriate, and stable, I'm not even drawn to him. I don't get it. I want one thing but don't like it when I get it."

That's because *getting* and *having* are two different things. For many, the quest is an end in itself. Perfectionists constantly search for that elusive nirvana. For others, the state of wanting is familiar, but having and enjoying are unknowns. These people stick to the pursuit or struggle but do not allow themselves to enjoy the reward, even when they know it's at their fingertips.

Then there are those who have a deep, inner longing to be happy. Their achievements are an attempt to experience that contentment. Unfortunately, another cruise, a better wardrobe, one more prestigious promotion or appointment, another community award, a financial bonus or two, or a new car won't fill that inner void.

Many people are looking for the solution in the wrong place. Look inside yourself to see what's there, beyond the achievements and possessions. See what's good and relish it, then assess your spiritual life. If you've neglected it, chances are that deep longing has been growing stronger as a result. Once you begin to satisfy it, things will begin to be "enough" and life will take on a new perspective.

Focus on what you truly want and what really matters to you, then allow yourself to receive it. It means letting go of the control and power of searching in order to find the relief, simplicity and peace that comes with having and being. It also means accepting yourself, accepting others, and accepting the joys and troubles of simply being human.

Let things happen, then revel in the outcome you desire (or try to appreciate the outcome you didn't expect). Wanting won't seem as enticing once you experience the contentment and satisfaction of having and knowing yourself instead.

Chapter 22

Beyond Your Control

Guilt.

For many people, it's more than just another emotion; it's a constant companion. While guilt compels you to do some things, it can more often keep you from accomplishing others. Some people even feel guilty about feeling guilty or guiltier yet for not feeling guilty enough!

Worry is as futile as guilt. Worriers spend so much of their time and energy focusing on their fear of what might happen in the future, they miss enjoying the present.

Guilt and worry are two of the biggest enemies of minority professionals, especially women. Both emotions take an extraordinary amount of time and produce no tangible, worthwhile, lasting results. Guilt and worry also make people tired and irritable. Worse yet, time spent with a guilty person or a worrier is usually a drag.

Guilt and worry are connected, and professional minority women are particularly prone to severe cases. The cycle of guilt and worry is exhausting, but it can be broken.

Most professional women have long histories of regret at past mistakes and fear of making new ones. Certain assumptions feed guilt and worry through the years. A discussion of some of the most common follows. Don't worry—you can change these beliefs, if you really want to.

"I Am not Enough"

The corollary to this belief is that nothing you do is enough, either. Most people don't usually tell each other directly that another person is inadequate or that he just doesn't cut it. But in one way or another, people pick up that message early in life.

Parental criticisms such as, "Bobby, look at this report card! Why can't you be more like your brother?" can sometimes turn into a self-statement that says, "I can't do anything right!" Comments such as these become firmly ingrained by age 9 and are almost irretractible by age 29. With every mistake, feelings of guilt begin to mount. The catch is that the more risks you take, the more you progress, the greater your chances are of erring and increasing your load of guilt.

If you're not regretting past mistakes, you might be prone to worrying about future errors. "I've never done this job before, and I don't know everything about it. I don't know if I can do it." This plays harmony to the melody of "You're Not Enough."

Tanya had been on the job for a year when her first child was born. "I can't handle this," she fretted. "I'm afraid my job will suffer and so will my baby. I just want to do it right. I don't want to mess things up."

Besides the lack of trust in her ability to handle this new life situation, Tanya was operating on the second-most-common guilt-and-worry producing assumption among minorities, especially women.

Sometimes minorities who were raised in areas without abundant resources interpret, incorrectly, that *they* are not enough. The cycle of acquiring more possessions to be "more" as a person feeds low self-esteem and the vicious cycles of guilt and worry.

"I Must Be Perfect"

Talk about a set-up! If you were raised with impossible standards and you continue to impose them on yourself, watch out. You're in for a great case of guilt and worry. No one is perfect at anything, and you needn't be a exception.

Isabel ran herself ragged—up early to leave the house spotless and everything ready for dinner. On to the office, with no lunch hour, where she tried to get "everything" done, then back home to tend to her family. But perfectly balanced home-cooked meals every night ("That's the way he likes them"), an impeccably clean house (your home is your castle), and model children (wouldn't it be nice?) are unreasonable expectations for the working woman to consistently accomplish all by herself.

If you do expect perfection, you're doomed to constant worry. Eventually you'll realize your fears.

"I Must Always Be Productive"

Children of workaholics, beware! If you were taught as a child that your time must always be spent "productively," you may be an adult who feels guilty about "not doing enough" and guiltier still about relaxing, if you even know how to relax! You probably also worry about wasting time and fret over getting "It" done.

But the question of what is "enough" and what is "productive" are not necessarily the point. Sometimes taking care of yourself is the best thing you can do. Unfortunately, to the guilt-ridden worrier, it's the last consideration.

"If It's Enjoyable, It Must Be Bad"

If you believe this, you're on the track to Guilt City. You'll feel pangs of guilt if you enjoy what you're doing or if you believe that "fun" equals "bad." If you don't feel guilty already, perhaps you can worry that too much fun was never good, so you'll try not to enjoy yourself too much.

> "Congratulations, Celina!" her friend began. "You completed the biggest assignment yet, and management loved it. We should celebrate and . . ."
> "I don't know about that," Celina interrupted. "There are so many things left to do. I don't dare take a break, or they'll think I'm goofing off.

Minorities raised in an ultraconservative area often develop an extreme work ethic that deprives them of enjoying the benefits of their work. In their experiences enjoyment is not only different; it's bad. A minority professional has many ways of ensuring that work isn't fun at all.

"Good Things Only Come with Hard Work"

A variation of the "enjoyable equals bad" logic, the idea that we must work hard for anything to be of value, causes stress overload and a sense of guilt or confusion if something good comes easily.

> "I don't get it," said Jesse. "Just when I was needing a new contract to increase my business, one came in. I wonder what the catch is. I didn't work for it at all!"

— — —

Ruth had a similar attitude, but she played it out in her personal relationships. Any man who was too kind, too attentive, or too available didn't present a challenge to her, so she wasn't interested. As a result, her life was filled with men who were "interesting" but with whom she would never form a lasting relationship.

It's important to remember that hard work doesn't guarantee anything. Sometimes the best things are yours just for the asking.

"Calm, Peace, and Satisfaction Are Fleeting"

With concerted effort, peace can be attained despite any difficulties that may arise. Many people become so hooked on the emotional high of crises or turmoil that serenity seems unnatural by comparison. In fact, some manufacture trouble just to keep the frenzy going and to ensure that peace is temporary. For them, calm causes worry ("What will happen next?") and satisfaction breeds guilt ("I'm too happy with my job. What did I do to deserve something so nice?").

> "This is heaven," Darlene thought, as she rested her feet on the coffee table. "The kids are off to school. I've got a free day, and the bills are paid. Of course, by noon, something upsetting will probably happen. The other contract's due at work, my kid's grades are being sent, and I've got a feeling the water heater is about to die."

If you were raised, as many minority professionals are, in an atmosphere of want, struggle, and tension, calm, peace, and satisfaction have historically been fleeting. It takes high self-esteem and a great deal of self-awareness to let serenity, not chaos, be a natural way of living. This is the struggle many minorities face or perpetuate.

"Nothing Is Forever"

Talk about worry and guilt! How can you build a successful career or develop lasting relationships if you can't count on anyone? Ironically, many people who believe that nothing is forever also believe that they should forever be consistent, unchanging, and undaunted. They leave little margin for personal change. The rest of the world may seem elusive and undependable to the person who isn't flexible and won't bend with it.

YOU *CAN* MAKE CHANGES

Worrying doesn't protect against misfortune, and guilt is such a drain that you really need to stop it. There are some things you can do to take control of your life.

First, check the payoffs. If you feel guilty enough about something, maybe you won't force yourself to change or to tackle something new. If you feel guilty over one failed relationship, why try another? If you didn't get promoted the last time around, maybe you figure you don't need to try again. Guilt might actually be serving as a wall to protect you from moving forward to take risks.

If nothing else, maybe you expect your guilt to engender some pity (though others rarely care), or perhaps it will persuade someone else to make decisions for you. Most people would like someone to take care of them sometimes, if only for a while. Playing helpless might work occasionally, but asking for help directly is much more efficient.

Second, ask yourself whether you listen to the right people. Don't believe everything you hear. Even "authorities," self-proclaimed or otherwise, can miss the mark, so consider alternatives.

Third, you may be wrong in your thinking. The way you view yourself isn't necessarily accurate. Maybe there are some things you dislike about yourself, but you don't view yourself as thoroughly bad in the process. Fat thighs doesn't mean the end of a relationship. One mistake on the job doesn't mean you're thoroughly incompetent. The punishment should fit the crime; chances are your offenses are more imagined than real. So go ahead. Lighten up!

"Rewards" of Worrying

Worrying gives people something to do. Some people can play so many possible scenarios in their minds, they feel as though they've been through everything already when they haven't actually done a thing!

Worry depletes energy that could otherwise be spent on action. But worriers can feel justified or smug, believing they care more than those who don't worry as much. Often worriers are resentful of others because they perceive that others don't "do" as much about things as they do. All this is just an illusion, because all the activity was in their minds.

Release Yourself from Guilt and Worry

Start by examining some of your false assumptions and possible related payoffs. Focus on the present and determine what you can and cannot control. Do what you can manage and set aside what you can't. You don't need to do it all. You don't need to do it perfectly, either. Quiet the eternal critic that feeds your negative feelings.

Try granting yourself permission to enjoy things and to make mistakes. The old "Shame on You!" need not become a guilty "Shame on Me!" Welcome yourself to the human race, imperfect as it is. It will come as a great relief.

Look to yourself for answers and satisfaction. You deserve success and serenity—guilt free. Focus on your thoughts, develop your self-confidence, build trust in a Higher Power, and let go. Then watch the worry go too.

As a minority professional, you must understand that being successful does not make you less ethnic, less feminine, or less like your minority counterparts. If anything, it broadens your experience—guilt- and worry-free.

You're not Always in Charge

Professionals are usually "take charge" people. When they sense that something isn't going as planned, they often try to get it to change its course. Control—getting things to go your way—is so strongly ingrained and rewarded among professionals that it seems as if it's the natural thing to do. But part of maturity is learning what you can control, personally and professionally, and what you can't. There are even some things you really *shouldn't* control.

If you're stuck in a cycle of trying to control too many things in your life, you probably experience a lot of frustration. Letting go of the need to control frees you from that continual undercurrent of tension and the gnawing feeling of not having a good grasp on things.

Start by determining what areas in your personal and professional life are causing you concern or frustration. If your boss is overly critical, if you fear that the contract won't be approved, if you don't like the way someone else is behaving, chances are you're trying to get things to go your way. Ask yourself what final results you'd like to see in a given situation. If it's a person's response or the outcome of a situation or event, keep reading.

Ask yourself who needs to change the situation. If you're not the answer but you're trying to do it anyway, you're setting yourself up for a round of negative feelings based on a need to control. Look at your list again. Take charge of the area you're in charge of. If it requires changing anybody but you, it's not your responsibility.) Complete your own responsibilities as best you can; the rest is out of your hands.

Now comes the tough part. Let go of anything that is *not* your responsibility or that you cannot directly change. Allow someone else to take over—a coworker, your supervisor, the guy next door. The best source to trust is a Higher Power, because you'll always get a response and things will always work out—maybe not necessarily as you wished, but as they should.

If you're having a difficult time letting go, chances are you're afraid and not trusting that things will work out for the best. Try to develop your faith in others, in the universe, in the order of things. The greater your faith and trust, the less your worry and need to control.

If you really take charge of just your own responsibilities, you'll have your hands full anyway. The outcome of all those other things is usually better than we originally expected.

Chapter 23

Time for a Change?

You know the feeling—you'd love to quit your job but you feel you can't. Your instincts tell you it's time to move on, but for some elusive reason you hang on instead. Face it. Your job is holding you hostage.

Unlike the abrupt capture of a political hostage, a hostage in the work place is slowly and subtly seduced into captivity. An employee who hasn't been alert to the danger signs along the way can begin to feel increasingly trapped.

On the surface, a work situation might appear ideal—respectable pay, good benefits, reasonable challenges. Things start out fine. In time, these attractive features can actually become the bonds that tie you to your position. The best way to elude your potential captors is to understand and remember that company or corporate philosophy is based on three fundamental premises:

□ Decisions are based on the bottom line.

□ Company loyalty is paramount.

□ Employees are dispensable.

SIGNS OF BEING HELD HOSTAGE BY A JOB

A potential job hostage is easy to identify. He is usually the one focused solely on his own career ambitions, performance, and growth. He is so busy keeping his eye on the ball that he can't watch the rest of the game. Unfortunately, the corporate politics of the playing field can kill an aspiring professional.

Laura had graduated at the top of her class and worked as an intern at a major corporation for a couple of years, receiving rave reviews on her performance. Ready to move on, she accepted a newly created position as a technical assistant to the vice president for research and development. The vice president hired Laura without hesitation because she was bright and enthusiastic. All Laura wanted was to help develop new products; all the boss wanted was to look good.

Things went well for a few months. After Laura completed a major project, the company president took notice and let her boss know how pleased he was with her work. The president increasingly asked for her help on other special projects being considered by upper management.

Laura was thrilled, but her boss wasn't. Her first mistake was keeping her eye too much on product development and not enough on her boss. She didn't notice that he felt threatened by her. He feared she would eventually take over his job.

She became the victim of sabotage. Her boss criticized nearly all her work. She failed to receive memos; she was excluded from office parties. It wasn't long before rumors about her started to circulate. She noticed the change but brushed it off. That was her second mistake.

Laura had believed her performance and determination were enough to carry her through. But the more she tried, the harder her job became. Within six months, Laura was miserable. She felt isolated, stymied, and stuck. She knew it was best to quit, but she couldn't bring herself to do it. The longer she stayed, the worse she felt.

Professionals often stay long after they know it's time to leave or permit themselves to be held captive by a job because of hope. Laura took the job believing this "was it," this was where she was going to make her mark. Like many dedicated professionals, she hoped for acceptance and recognition. She wanted to make a difference.

> Margarita completed her graduate degree in counseling and was prepared to work in the community. She found what seemed like an ideal job working in a Hispanic agency, counseling families and doing some educational work.
> "The management, clients, and staff are all Hispanic," she reasoned, "so I should be able to do well here."
> Margarita did so well that her supervisor felt threatened by her. She gave Margarita tougher cases and provided little assistance in handling them. Margarita was given few educational assignments (her real joy), but her caseload grew larger. Working harder and harder, Margarita still hoped for recognition, a sense of belonging, and advancement.

Like many other minority professionals, Margarita wanted to "make a difference." It took her a long time to realize it wouldn't happen here.

When recognition and the rewards minority professionals seek are not forthcoming, a professional often believes all he needs to do is try harder. That's when the employee gets hooked, just like a gambler. He tries harder and harder, and occasionally it pays off. A bonus, a memo or even a backhanded compliment becomes a sign of hope. All he needs to do is keep trying.

Examining our two examples, we see that Laura was trapped by her narrow definition of where and how she wanted to achieve her goals. She believed so firmly that she had to hold her position with that particular company that she failed to recognize she had options. Margarita fell into the same trap.

Professionals sometimes lament that they can't leave even a hopeless job because they'll never find another job like it. (Ideally, they won't!) What they're really saying is they see only one option, their current job situation. The result is a feeling of being eternally stuck.

Sometimes professionals rationalize staying in a bad work situation because they can't afford to quit. They have become accustomed to a certain lifestyle tied to the earnings, status, and perks of a specific job. Leaving that job might mean losing club memberships, extra vehicles, paid vacations, and a high level of living. If those are important, or if you are in debt, quitting doesn't seem to be a realistic option. Money is the captor.

Ironically, while a job might provide these comforts, the quality of life for a job hostage is dismal. Her work atmosphere is often tense and restrictive. Such employees often complain that they're not treated with basic human respect. Conflict is the norm and suspicion is pervasive. People have an increasingly limited sense of freedom. These feelings can be very contagious; they can make an entire office feel trapped.

Minority professionals may become hostages to their jobs for other reasons. If you're in a field in which there are few other people of a similar background, it may feel intimidating to "get out there" and find something more suitable if you don't have a lot of "connections." The token minority may like the status of being "the only" one getting attention and being included in various activities, but simultaneously dislike the isolation the position brings.

Minorities raised with a very traditional background sometimes feel disloyal leaving a job that once held positive things for them. Competition may still cause uneasy feelings, so that a professional will put off searching for a new job out of apprehension. Minority professionals often become hostage to their jobs for the same reasons non-minorities may—money, complacency, fixed ideas on how things should be. But minorities may face these things alone, with little guidance from a mentor and few role models to emulate. When you don't know what to do, you may stay right where you are, like it or not.

Sometimes minority professionals who are job hostages remain where they are because they fear disappointing other minorities or because they might prove non-minorities "right."

> "I just hate to leave this position," Leslie began. "I'm the first woman CEO, and everyone's been waiting for me to fail. If I quit, that's what they'll think. All the men can say, 'I told you a female couldn't handle the pressure!'"

The pressure of saving face, avoiding disappointing others, or proving a point is costly.

"My parents will be so disappointed."

"How can I look other blacks in the face if I quit?"

"If I leave, it'll take years before they fill the position with another minority again."

These are all compelling reasons to stay in a position, even if you're unhappy. But all have one thing in common: they don't consider the well-being of the individual. Ironically, an unhappy employee can end up doing more damage in the long run by conveying a negative attitude than he would have had if he had left the job when it was "time."

The price a person pays for being held hostage by a job is high. It is physical and emotional extortion. You know how it goes. On weekday mornings you wake up exhausted. Dutifully, you get ready for work, but the anxiety is gnawing at your stomach, neck, or lower back. Your head starts to throb. You make a fleeting wish that something would happen so you wouldn't have to go to the office. On the way to work you're distracted, running scenarios through your mind and rehearsing how you'll handle things "next" time. You enter the building filled with dread. An hour seems like an eternity. Trips to the water cooler or to the employee lounge offer little relief. You feel so overwhelmed and oppressed that the only thing you can think clearly about is what time you get to go home.

These feelings of oppression can take their toll on your health. Colitis, ulcers, heart palpitations, dizziness, backaches, muscular stiffness in the neck and shoulders, unusual rashes, allergies, and headaches may come and go. An unhappy employee often seems to have one illness after another. Piece by piece, his body gives in to his ailing spirit.

Employees in a bad work situation often report being tired. Even after a good night's sleep they may wake up feeling tired, with little energy. This "fatigueability" is the tendency for someone under stress to tire easily, whether or not she has done enough work to warrant fatigue. Simply showing up for work takes great effort.

Emotionally, a bad work situation exacts a high price. Af first, the unhappy person begins to derive less and less satisfaction from her work. As the job situation worsens, other areas of life are affected as well. Ultimately, few things in life seem worth the effort.

Friends and family feel it too. Complaints about work spill into complaints about home. Formerly pleasant events become chores, and nothing seems quite right, even with loved ones. If a bad job scene is allowed to drag on long enough, family and friends follow the corporate saga and can begin to predict the next crisis. After awhile, everyone wishes the beleaguered employee would quit. Negative messages from others to the worker begin to seep in, and the person begins to doubt his own abilities. If the situation continues, the job hostage questions his competence and his self-worth.

This low self-concept invades other areas of life. The person in the job-hostage situation might begin to reason, "If I can't be a competent professional, how can I possibly be a good spouse or parent?" "How can I possibly represent minorities well if I can't do this?" He may begin to shy away from meeting new contacts or tackling new challenges. It would be safer to avoid these things, he tells himself, because he might "blow it," just like at work.

Many job hostages simply keep on trying, at least for a time. They might alter their approach, change their product, offer suggestions or try to reason with those at work. When a discouraged employee has tried everything without effecting much change, he concludes he is helpless, that nothing he does makes a difference. Such an employee may decide, "Oh, well, it doesn't matter. Nothing matters. Why try?"

With that, the job hostage admits he is stuck and powerless, and he gives in to his captors. That's why job hostages are depressed. Their freedom is curtailed and their self-esteem is low. They lack hope, have recurring self-doubts, and find it nearly impossible to function as before.

Personal finances can also take a beating when someone is stuck in a miserable job. If earnings are based on performance, as they are in sales and some kinds of production, income will probably decrease as an employee's unhappiness increases. As work performance slows down, so does income.

Sometimes people spend money in an attempt to feel better. Unhappy employees often believe that extended vacations, boats or cars, and new wardrobes will make working "worth it" and help them feel better. Spending does help temporarily, and that's the problem. Like a gambler or other addict, the job hostage can buy something, feel better, then feel worse, and buy something else. Spending doesn't cure the problem; it worsens it.

SOME SOLUTIONS TO THE PROBLEM

You can take action to remedy a job-hostage situation before you wreck your health, ruin your finances, lose your friends, alienate your family, and sink into depression.

To avoid being held hostage by your job, take a few precautions when you start a new position. Play the waiting game. Figure out the players, the rules, the winners, and the losers before making your move. Study the corporate politics before stepping blindly into an untenable situation. Determine who holds formal and informal power—who holds the title versus who holds the real clout. Keep your work goal in mind, but understand that you must work within the reality of that situation.

In setting a work goal, try initially to capture the essence of what you want rather than the specifics. Figure out which aspects of work are most important and what you want to accomplish. Then look for situations to fulfill your goals. Instead of setting your mind on only one position with a certain company, keep in mind the general "feel" of the work you want and look for a place to carry it out. Someone who wants to work with people, make a difference to others, and continue learning could be a teacher, a librarian, or even a career counselor.

This approach to achievement in work can help you remember your goals and options. You'll be much less likely to feel trapped by a job if you focus on what you want rather than a narrow definition of where and how it must be.

Try this if you are having trouble extracting yourself from a bad work situation out of fear that it's the only job that will fulfill what you've outlined for yourself. You can probably accomplish what you want elsewhere. It might be in a different way and in a different setting. You actually might end up freer to do your work and with fewer hassles. Chapter 2, page 17, contains a discussion on creating your vision of work and your future. The same principles also apply to moving within your career.

Watch your assumptions about work, success, and colleague support. Chapter 9, page 79, looks at the "right moves" and the mistakes minorities can make to sabotage their careers. If you expect help when it won't be forthcoming, seek recognition when it won't be given, or expect special treatment because of your minority status, look again. Those assumptions and the ideas outlined in this chapter can hold you hostage in a job for a long time.

Take a close look at how much power you allow your job to hold over you. If someone else dictates how you feel about yourself and how much satisfaction you derive from your work or your life in general, perhaps you've handed over control. It helps to know who is really the captor.

Chapter 24

The Other Side of the Coin— Managing Minority Employees

Cultural diversity and the changing work force may be the biggest challenges to managers and employers in the future. According to recent studies, the following trends have been noted:

□ Professional and non-professional minority employees will some day make up the majority of the work force.

□ More employees than ever before will be older.

□ Women may outnumber men.

What does this mean for management? The flexibility to understand and appreciate varied backgrounds, and a tolerance for continued change, will be more important than ever.

This chapter looks at the challenges of dealing with the changing work force of the future, the assumptions that could get in your way, and some positive approaches to potential problems.

CHALLENGES OF DEALING WITH A MINORITY WORK FORCE

The most compelling, yet subtle, challenge in working with a predominantly ethnic-minority, female, older work force will be people's reactions—yours and theirs.

If you're a non-minority manager, you may find differences in the way people approach their work, how they communicate with each other, and how they respond to you. Fear, frustration, loneliness, intolerance, impatience, and wishing you could return to the "good old days" are common feelings among non-minority professionals managing groups of minority employees. If you can see this challenge as an *opportunity*, you might also feel exhilarated and hopeful.

Knowing the rules and being willing to change them will be your greatest challenges as a manager. You may have been following a traditional set of work rules for years, rules from the "old boy network" by which you knew how to handle different situations. Whether in the boardroom or on the assembly line or golf course, you could get the job done by knowing how to set goals, compete, and communicate.

With a non-minority work force, the rules may start to change, albeit subtly. Goals will become task-oriented and socially oriented. Relationships will be very important, if not primary, to employees. Employees will be more apt to cooperate with each other instead of competing. Communication styles will also vary, depending on employees' backgrounds. If you can adapt the rules to match the changing work force rather than hammering the new work force to meet the old rules, you'll be way ahead of the game.

Building cohesion amidst diversity will come next. People often focus on *differences* between people. Participative management and teamwork within a diverse work force will require identifying and building on *similarities*.

Understanding who you're dealing with may be one of your greatest challenges. If you understand, accept, and maybe even appreciate the diversity and backgrounds of the people you work with, many "problems" will be reduced to manageable situations. Having a sense of a non-minority's history—ancestry, cultural backgrounds, defeats, victories, and continuing struggles in different areas of life—will be the key to knowing how people think, and it will help you work with them more effectively.

Beyond their history, discover how your minority workers view themselves now—their sense of empowerment, their current situation, their world view. These things will tell you how to manage and build the team effectively. Also important is their hope for the future. If quality child care, enough money for education, and a secure family life are most important, you'll know which incentives and benefits to provide.

Perhaps the greatest challenge to a non-minority manager supervising a diverse work force is broadening your approach, expanding your horizons, and allowing yourself to grow in self-understanding. If you know who you are and what's important to you, it will be easier to lead a team, diverse as it may be. Each experience will enrich your sense of self and help it grow. If you can change as your work force changes, meet the challenges presented by a diverse group of employees, and allow yourself to give beyond your previously established limits, what you receive will far outweigh your expectations.

EXAMINE YOUR ASSUMPTIONS

Minority and non-minority managers bring to their supervisory situation a set of assumptions by which they approach the job and handle their work team to get a job done. Some of the following assumptions are often held by those who work with a diverse or minority work force. Examining and changing some assumptions may help you to be more effective as a manager.

All Minorities Are the Same

This is a dangerous assumption. For example, within "Hispanics" you have Mexicans, Mexican-Americans, Puerto Ricans, Cubans, Central Americans, South Americans, and Iberians. Blacks from southern rural settings are different from those who come from large northern cities. Women are as varied as men.

A person's economic background, the ways and places in which he was raised, and his level of education also largely determine how that individual views the world of work and how he performs with others. If you understand this, you'll realize you are truly dealing with a *diverse* work force!

What's Important to You Is Important to Your Employees

Managers and supervisors often reward people on the job in the same way people sometimes shop for gifts: they find something they really like, then give it to the other person. The recipient may or may not share the same tastes.

Reinforcement is important to employees, so you need to make sure the rewards you use with them will hit the mark. You may think that what your workers truly want is more money. That may be true, but check it out. Maybe a working mother really wants flexible hours or assistance with child care. Maybe an older employee wants a sabbatical to approach a new task or return to school.

None of these things may be personally rewarding for you as a manager, but if it meets the needs of your workers, you'll be right on target.

Minorities Are Incompetent Until They Prove Otherwise

Whether or not supervisors and coworkers will admit it, this is often the approach they take when a minority or "first" takes a new position on the job.

"Women have never worked here, so we'll have to see if they can handle the job."

"We've never had a black in that position, so we're going to see how he gets along with everyone else."

"This position has usually been filled by an older person. We'll have to see what this energetic young kid fresh out of college can do."

With non-minority employees, people typically assume that if you've been given a job, you're qualified to hold the position. A non-minority can go about doing his work more calmly, not having to "prove" himself until a mistake is made. A minority, on the other hand, is always on the testing ground, vigilant against mistakes and fearful that all minorities will be labeled incompetent if he or she is anything less than perfect.

Ways You Measure Performance for Minority Employees May not Be the Same as for Non-minority Employees

While managers may attest otherwise, there are often different standards by which minorities are evaluated. A minority's work performance usually receives closer scrutiny, especially if she is "the first" to hold a given position. People will watch to see how that person handles the

231

pressure, whether she makes mistakes and how she gets along with coworkers. Often the minority employee is put in the position of having to work twice as hard to get half as far.

Receiving a Good Performance Evaluation Doesn't Mean You're Working Well

Minority professionals often work extremely hard to prove themselves and to succeed in the work place. Good performance evaluations of their technical competence are not that unusual. If you look further, you may find that these minority professionals are not working well with others. If they're isolated or scrutinized, working extraordinary hours, and being excluded from social events, the minority employee may actually not be working or interacting very well with non-minority coworkers.

A woman who is the only female in an all-male work group may turn out huge amounts of quality work. But she doesn't get included in the lunch hour discussions, isn't "in" on the grapevine gossip, and is isolated in almost every way from her male counterparts. She may be getting the technical aspects of the job done effectively and efficiently, but the interactional part of her work is of poor quality . . . and that affects the team.

Minorities Have as Good a Chance of Succeeding and Rising in the Corporation as Anyone Else

This may be true where you're a manager, but minorities have been hitting the "glass ceiling" for years. It appears that you can climb to the top: upper management says so, it looks like it, and you work like crazy to get there. But somehow, you never get past a certain point—the glass ceiling.

"Our company has done extremely well in placing minorities in management positions . . ." the CEO began.

"*Midmanagement* positions," thought a dozen or so women who were in the audience. "We have six female assistant vice presidents, but no one has made it past that level. What's it going to take to get any higher on the ladder?"

Minorities Have Been Promoted into Management Positions Equally

A closer look at employment rosters and organizational charts of some corporations that have placed many minorities in management positions reveals that white women predominantly hold those positions. While women are classified as a minority, it still leaves the company without an ethnically or racially integrated work force. You might have more women at the top, but you still have an all-white decision-making structure.

Determine whether or not you're really promoting minorities of all types—ethnic minorities, older employees, *and* women. Then you can determine how equal the treatment has really been.

DILEMMAS MANAGERS FACE

Even if your assumptions are clear and positive, even if you have every intention of having your work force balanced, even if you try all kinds of methods for building a cooperative team, as a manager of a diverse work force you may face many problems and dilemmas. Here are some of the common problems managers face when working with minorities.

*You May Be Told to Diversify Your Work Force at a Higher Level,
But You Claim You Can't Find "Qualified Minorities" to Fill the
Positions*

On the surface, it may appear that you can't find any women
or ethnic minorities to fill upper-management positions in
your corporation. Because many minority groups—especially ethnic minorities—have historically had limited numbers
seeking higher education, you may have a smaller pool of
candidates from which to draw, especially compared to the
number of non-minorities who are available.

Take a look at your incentives, how "minority friendly"
the corporate environment is, and whether upper management is truly dedicated—not merely giving lip service—to
diversifying the work force at the mid and upper-management levels. If the incentives, attitudes, and commitments are
right, keep looking for those minorities. You'll have to build a
special network or use some special outreach techniques to
reach minorities, but you're bound to attract them.

*Some Minority Employees May Use Their Minority Status as a
Weapon to Threaten or Blackmail a Manager*

You can't say it won't happen, any more than you can say a
non-minority member won't sue over some kind of unfair
treatment. Take these three steps first.

□ Determine whether the person has been placed in a
job that is technically appropriate for her.

□ Examine the attitudes of the person's coworkers.

□ Determine whether you have treated the employee
justly, based on the same assumptions you use with
non-minority employees.

Only after you follow these steps will you be in a position to know whether the person is legitimately raising a problem issue or if she is using her minority status as a smokescreen or threat. If that threat is being posed, you may need to seek assistance or advice from your human resources office or the legal department.

Giving a Chance to One Minority Means You'll Have to Do the Same for All Minorities

If you grant an opportunity to one minority, it will give a definite message to all others—that you're willing to do so. It's only natural for them to seek the same opportunity for themselves.

If you have a plan for diversifying your work force, you can accomplish it one position at a time. It can't be done overnight, but progress can be made steadily.

APPROACHES TO MANAGING A DIVERSE WORK FORCE EFFECTIVELY

As a manager, you will experience great challenges in working with a group of people with varied backgrounds, interests, ages, attitudes, and styles. Below are some guidelines for effectively managing that challenge.

Ask Yourself Whether You Have a Genuine Commitment to Working Effectively with a Diverse Work Force

Just as line employees resist change, so does management. It takes a great deal more energy, creativity, and tenacity to manage a diverse work force, at least in the beginning. Honestly assess whether you are really positive and accepting of that challenge. If you're not, you'll be fighting your own resistance and resistance from others.

Be Positive in Your Interactions

Whatever you decide your experience will be in meeting the challenges of a diversified work force, that's probably what you'll experience. Do you approach your management job positively in a diversified work force? Ask yourself whether you are honestly treating your minority employees the same way you treat their non-minority counterparts.

If you place the same expectations on them and are open to communication, they'll know it and act accordingly. If they sense that you're being condescending, that you feel imposed upon, or that you're against dealing positively with the changing work force, you'll get resistance in return.

Stay Focused on Your Need to Interact Successfully with Minority Employees

Wishing won't make all these changes go away. You need to get the team to work together, so focus on that task. Fear and negative assumptions will dissipate, and things being taken "personally" will be minimized, if you're keen on communicating well and getting the job done efficiently and effectively.

Be Familiar with Your Work and Communication Style and Theirs

You might like to hit the ground running in the morning, working a straight, fixed number of hours. Women employees may need to come in later and have flexible hours because of child-care responsibilities. You may like to give assignments and have employees work independently. Some ethnic minorities and women might better accomplish their tasks as a group. You may say what's on your mind directly, without mincing words. Your employees might be more indirect; you may feel as if they "beat around the bush."

Learn to listen, observe, and understand their point of view. Be familiar with your own and see how the two mesh. You can adjust your own approach and expectations to get through to others if you're aware of people's styles of work and communication.

Find Out What You Have in Common

It's easy to see how people are different. In a work force, that only divides the team. Most people love to talk about their children, whether it's a "wonder child" firstborn or a difficult teenager. They enjoy sports or the arts or gardening. They want a nice life, just as you do. They generally want to do a good job.

Look for similarities in the goals, interests, and even dislikes you both hold. You'll minimize some of the differences between you.

Don't Judge Another Person Before You Get to Know Him

If someone tells you all Hispanics are overemotional and impulsive, you might start out with that mindset before you even hire one! In reality, your source of information might have a biased view of Hispanics based on his own experience, preferences, needs, or style.

If a man tells you having women in management is difficult, maybe you're talking to someone who doesn't care for women, feels that only men should be making decisions, or has had a bad experience with a women making decisions. Be

237

careful whom you listen to. You should really depend only on your *own* intuition.

Approach Each Minority Employee as a Person Who Will Grant You a New Opportunity

You never know when the person you're dealing with will bring a wealth of technical skill and creativity for solving old problems to the job. If nothing else, each person you encounter—minority or non-minority—can teach you something about yourself.

Envision Getting What You Want

If you aim at getting the job done in a productive, enjoyable way, you'll probably have the patience to see how people interact and you'll be able to adapt your style and expectations to get a job done. You may not get things done in the same way you did in the past, but you may get them done better!

Bibliography

A Way of Life and Selected Writings of Sir William Osler (12 July 1849 to 29 December 1919). New York: Dover Publications, 1951.

Alcoholics Anonymous: The Story of How Many Thousands of Men and Women Have Recovered from Alcoholism. New York: Alcoholics Anonymous World Services, 1976.

Foster, Richard J. *Celebration of Discipline: The Path to Spiritual Growth.* San Francisco: Harper & Row, 1978.

Fox, Emmet. *Power Through Constructive Thinking.* San Francisco: Harper & Row, 1940.

Merton, Thomas. *No Man Is An Island.* San Diego, Harcourt Brace Jovanovich, 1983.

Peck, M. Scott. *The Road Less Traveled: A New Psychology of Love, Traditional Values and Spiritual Growth.* New York: Simon & Schuster, 1978.

Phelps, Janice K. and Nourse, Alan E. *The Hidden Addiction and How to Get Free*. Boston: Little, Brown and Co., 1986.

Ross, Ruth. *Prospering Woman: A Complete Guide to Achieving the Full, Abundant Life*. New York: Bantam Books, 1985.

Scheele, Adele M. *Skills for Success: A Guide to the Top*. New York: William Morrow & Co., Inc., 1979.

Velez, Carlos. Various speeches and workshops. Director, Bureau of Applied Research in Anthropology, University of Arizona, Tucson Arizona.

The Basics of Job Winning

The best way to obtain a better professional job is to contact the employer directly. Broad-based statistical studies by the Department of Labor show that job seekers have found employment more successfully by contacting employers directly, than by using any other method.

However, given the current diversity, and increased specialization of both industry and job tasks it is possible that in some situations other job seeking methods may prove at least equally successful. Three of the other most commonly used methods are: relying on personal contacts, using employment services, and following up help wanted advertisements. Many professionals have been successful in finding better jobs using one of these methods. However, the Direct Contact method has an overall success rate twice that of any other method and it has been successfully used by many more professionals. So unless you have specific reasons to believe that another method would work best for you, the Direct Contact method should form the foundation of your job search effort.

The Objective

With any business task, you must develop a strategy for meeting a goal. This is especially true when it comes to obtaining a better job. First you need to clearly define your objectives.

Setting your job objectives is better known as career planning (or life planning for those who wish to emphasize the importance of combining the two). Career planning has become a field of study in and of itself. Since most of our readers are probably well-entrenched in their career path, we will touch on career planning just briefly.

If you are thinking of choosing or switching careers, we particularly emphasize two things. First, choose a career where you will enjoy most of the day-to-day tasks. Sure, this sounds obvious, but most of us have at one point or another been attracted by a glamour industry or a prestigious sounding job without thinking of the most important consideration: Would we enjoy performing the everyday tasks the position entailed?

The second key consideration is that you are not merely choosing a career, but also a lifestyle. Career counselors indicate that one of the most common problems people encounter in job seeking is a lack of consideration for how well-suited they are for a particular position or career. For example, some people, attracted to management consulting by good salaries, early responsibility and high level corporate exposure, do not adapt well to the long hours, heavy travel demands, and the constant pressure to produce. So be sure to determine both for your career as a whole and for each position that you apply for, if you will easily adapt to both the day-to-day duties that the position entails and the working environment.

The Strategy

Assuming that you have now established your career objectives, the next step of the job search is to develop a strategy. If you don't take the time to develop a strategy and lay out a plan you will probably find yourself going in circles after several weeks making a random search for opportunities that always seem just beyond your reach.

Your strategy can have three simple elements:

1. Choosing a method of contacting employers.

2. Allocating your scarce resources (in most job searches the key scarce resource will be time, but financial considerations will become important in some searches too.)

3. Evaluating how the selected contact method is working and then considering adopting other methods.

We suggest you give serious consideration to using the Direct Contact method exclusively. However, we realize it is human nature to avoid putting all your eggs in one basket. So, if you prefer to use other methods as well, try to expend at least half your effort on the Direct Contact method, spending the rest on all of the other methods combined. Millions of other job seekers have already proven that Direct Contact has been twice as effective in obtaining employment, so why not benefit from their effort?

With your strategy in mind, the next step is to develop the details of the plan, or scheduling. Of course, job searches are not something that most people do regularly so it is difficult to estimate how long each step will take. Nonetheless, it is important to have a plan so that your effort can be allocated the way you have chosen, so that you can see yourself progressing, and to facilitate reconsideration of your chosen strategy.

It is important to have a realistic time frame in mind. If you will be job searching full-time, your search will probably take at least two months and very likely, substantially longer.

If you can only devote part-time effort, it will probably take four months.

You probably know a few people who seem to spend their whole lives searching for a better job in their part time. Don't be one of them. Once you begin your job search on a part-time basis, give it your whole-hearted effort. If you don't really feel like devoting a lot of energy to job seeking right now, then wait. Focus on enjoying your present position, performing your best on the job, and storing up energy for when you are really ready to begin your job search.

Those of you currently unemployed should remember that job hunting is tough work physically and emotionally. It is also intellectually demanding—requiring your best. So don't tire yourself out by working on your job campaign around the clock. It would be counter-productive. At the same time, be sure to discipline yourself. The most logical approach to time management is to keep your regular working hours.

For those of you who are still employed, job searching will be particularly tiring because it must be done in addition to your regular duties. So don't work yourself to the point where you show up to interviews appearing exhausted and slip behind at your current job. But don't be tempted to quit! The long hours are worth it—it is much easier to sell your skills from a position of strength (as someone currently employed).

If you are searching full-time and have decided to choose a mixture of contact methods, we recommend that you divide up each week allowing some time for each method. For instance, you might devote Mondays to following up newspaper ads because most of them appear in Sunday papers. Then you might devote Tuesdays, and Wednesday mornings to working and developing the personal contacts you have, in addition to trying a few employment services. Then you could devote the rest of the week to the Direct Contact method. This is just one plan that may succeed for you.

By trying several methods at once, job-searching will be more interesting for you, and you will be able to evaluate how promising each of the methods seems, altering your time allocation accordingly. Be very careful in your evaluation, however, and don't judge the success of a particular method just by the sheer number of interviews you obtain. Positions advertised in the newspaper, for instance, are likely to generate many more interviews per opening than positions that are filled without being advertised.

If you are searching part-time and decide to try several different contact methods, we recommend that you try them sequentially. You simply won't have enough time to put a meaningful amount of effort into more than one method at once. So decide how long your job search might take. (Only a guess, of course.) And then allocate so many weeks or months for each contact method you choose to use. (We suggest that you try Direct Contact first.)

If you are expected to be in your office during the business day, then you have an additional time problem to deal with. How can you work interviews into the business day? And if you work in an open office, how can you even call to set up interviews? As much as possible you should keep up the effort and the appearances on your present job. So maximize your use of the lunch hour, early in the morning and late in the afternoon for calling. If you really keep trying you will be surprised how often you will be able to reach the executive you are trying to contact during your out-of-office hours. The lunch hour for different executives will vary between 12 and 3. Also you can catch people as early as 8am and as late as 6pm on frequent occasions. Jot out a plan each night on how you will be using each minute of your precious lunch break.

Your inability to interview at any time other than lunch just might work to your advantage. If you can, try to set up as many interviews as possible for your lunch hour. This will go a long way to creating a relaxed rapport. (Who isn't happy when eating?) But be sure the interviews don't stray too far from the agenda on hand.

Lunchtime interviews will be much easier for the person with substantial career experience to obtain. People with less experience will often find that they have no alternative other than taking time off for interviewing. If you have to take time off, you have to take time off. But try to do this as little as possible. Usually you should take the whole day off so that it is not blatantly obvious that you are job searching. Try to schedule in at least two, or at the most three, interviews for the same day. (It is very difficult to maintain an optimum level of energy at more than three interviews in one day.) Explain to the interviewer why you might have to juggle your interview schedule—he/she should honor the respect you are showing your current employer by minimizing your days off and will probably appreciate the fact that another prospective employer is showing an interest in you.

Once again we need to emphasize if you are searching for a job, especially part-time, get out there and do the necessary tasks to the best of your ability and get it over with. Don't let your job search drag on endlessly.

Remember that all schedules are meant to be broken. The purpose of a schedule in your job search is not to rush you to your goal, its purpose is to map out the road ahead of you and evaluate the progress of your chosen strategy to date.

The Direct Contact Method

Once you have scheduled a time, you are ready to begin using the job search method that you have chosen. In the text we will restrict discussion to use of the Direct Contact method. Sideboards will comment briefly on developing your personal contacts and using newspaper advertisements.

The first step in preparing for Direct Contact is to develop a check list for categorizing the types of firms for which you would prefer working. You might categorize firms by their product line, their size, their customer-type (such as industrial or consumer), their growth prospects, or, of course by their geographical locations. Your list of important considerations might be very short. If it is, good! The shorter it is, the easier it will be to find appropriate firms.

Developing Your Contacts

Some career counselors feel that the best route to a better job is through somebody you already know or through somebody to whom you can be introduced. The counselors recommend you build your contact base beyond your current acquaintances by asking each one to introduce you, or refer you, to additional people in your field of interest.

The theory goes like this: You might start with 15 personal contacts, each of whom introduces you to 3 additional people, for a total 45 additional contacts. Then each of these people introduces you to three additional people which adds 135 additional contacts. Theoretically, you will soon know every person in the industry.

Of course, developing your personal contacts does not usually work quite as smoothly as the theory suggests because some people will not be able to introduce you to several relevant contacts. The further you stray from your initial contact base, the weaker your references may be. So, if you do try developing your own contacts, try to begin with as large an initial group of people you personally know as possible. Dig into your personal phone book and your holiday greeting card list and locate old classmates from school. Be particularly sure to approach people who perform your personal business such as your lawyer, accountant, banker, doctor, stockbroker, and insurance agent. These people develop a very broad contact base due to the nature of their professions. ■

Then try to decide at which firms you are most likely to be able to obtain employment. You might wish to consider to what degree your particular skills might be in demand, the degree of competition for employment, and the employment outlook at the firm.

Now you are ready to assemble your list of prospective employers. Build up your list to at least 100 prospects. Then separate your prospect list into three groups. The first tier of maybe 25 firms will be your primary target market, the second group of another 25 firms will be your secondary market, and remaining names you will keep in reserve.

This book will help you greatly in developing your prospect list. Refer to the primary employers section of this book. You will notice that employer listings are arranged according to industry, beginning with Accounting, followed by Advertising, and so on through to Utilities. If you know of a firm, but you're unsure of what industry it would be classified under, then refer to the alphabetically ordered employer index at the rear of the book to find the page number that the firm's listing appears on.

At this stage, once you have gotten your prospect list together and have an idea of the firms for which you might wish to work, it is best to get to work on your resume. Refer to formats of the sample resumes included in the Resumes and Cover Letters section that follows this chapter.

Once your resume is at the printer, begin research for the first batch of 25 prospective employers. You will want to determine whether you would be happy working at the firms you are researching and also get a better idea of what their employment needs might be. You also need to obtain enough information to sound highly informed about the company during phone conversations and in mail correspondence. But don't go all out on your research yet! At some of these firms you probably will not be able to arrange interviews, so save your big research effort until you start to arrange interviews. Nevertheless, you should plan to spend about 3 or 4 hours, on average, researching each firm. Do your research in batches to save time and energy. Go into one resource at a time and find out what you can about each of the 25 firms in the batch. Start with the easiest resources to use (such as this book.) Keep organized. Maintain a folder on each firm.

If you discover something that really disturbs you about the firm (i.e. perhaps they are about to close their only local office) or if you discover that your chances of getting a job there are practically nil (i.e. perhaps they just instituted a hiring freeze) then cross them off your prospect list.

If possible, supplement your research efforts with contacts to individuals who know the firm well. Ideally you should make an informal contact with someone at the particular firm, but often a contact at a direct competitor, or a major supplier or customer will be able to supply you with just as much information. At the very least try to obtain whatever printed information that the company has available, not just annual reports, but product brochures and anything else. The company might very well have printed information about career opportunities.

Getting The Interview

Now it is time to arrange an interview, time to make the Direct Contact. If you have read many books on job searching you have probably noticed that virtually all tell you to avoid the personnel office like the plague. It is said that the personnel office never hires people, they just screen out candidates. In some cases you may be able to identify and contact the appropriate manager with the authority to hire you. However, this will take a lot of time and effort in each case. Often you'll be bounced back to personnel. So we suggest that you begin your Direct Contact campaign through personnel offices. If it seems that in the firms on your prospect list that little hiring is done through personnel, you might consider an alternative course of action.

The three obvious means of initiating Direct Contact are:

- ▫ Showing up unannounced

- ▫ Phone calls

- ▫ Mail

Cross out the first one right away. You should never show up to seek a professional position without an appointment. Even if you are somehow lucky enough to obtain an interview, you will appear so unprofessional that you will not even be seriously considered.

Mail contact seems to be a good choice if you have not been in the job market for a while. You can take your time to prepare a careful letter, say exactly what you want, tuck your resume in, and then the addressee can read the material at leisure. But employers receive many resumes every day. Don't be surprised if you do not get a response to your inquiry. So don't spend weeks waiting for responses that never come. If you do send a cover letter, follow it up (or precede it) with a phone call. This will increase your impact, and underscore both your interest in the firm and the fact that you are familiar with it (because of the initial research you did.)

Another alternative is to make a "Cover Call." Your Cover Call should be just like your cover letter: concise. Your first sentence should interest the employer in you. Then try to subtly mention your familiarity with the firm. Don't be overbearing; keep your introduction to three sentences or less. Be pleasant, self confident and relaxed. This will greatly increase the chances of the person at the other end of the line developing the conversation. But don't press. When you are asked to follow up "with something in the mail" don't try to prolong the conversation once it has ended. Don't ask what they want to receive in the mail. Always send your resume and a highly

Don't Bother with Mass Mailing or Barrages Of Phone Calls

Direct Contact does not mean burying every firm within a hundred miles with mail and phone calls. Mass mailings rarely work in the job hunt. This also applies to those letters that are personalized — but dehumanized — on an automatic typewriter. Don't waste your time or money on such a project; you will fool no one but yourself.

The worst part of sending out mass mailings or making unplanned phone calls is that you are likely to be remembered as someone with little genuine interest in the firm, as someone who lacks sincerity, and as somebody that nobody wants to hire.

Help Wanted Advertisements

Only a small fraction of professional job openings are advertised. Yet a majority of job seekers—and a lot of people not in the job market—spend a lot of time studying the help wanted ads. As a result, the competition for advertised openings is often much more severe.

A moderate-sized Manhattan employer told us about an experience advertising in the help wanted section of a major Sunday newspaper:

It was a disaster. We had over 500 responses from this relatively small ad in just one week. We have only two phone lines in this office and one was totally knocked out. We'll never advertise for professional help again.

If you insist on following up on help wanted ads, then research a firm before you reply to an ad so that you can ascertain if you would be a suitable candidate and that you would enjoy working at a particular firm. Also such preliminary research might help to separate you from all of the other professionals responding to that ad, many of whom will only have a passing interest in the opportunity. That said, your chances of obtaining a job through the want-ads are still much smaller than they are if you use the Direct Contact method. ■

personalized follow-up letter, reminding the addressee of the phone conversation. Always include a cover letter even if you are requested to send a resume. (It is assumed that you will send a cover letter too.)

Unless you are in telephone sales, making smooth and relaxed cover calls will probably not come easily. Practice them on your own and then with your friends or relatives (friends are likely to be more objective and hence, better participants.)

If you obtain an interview over the telephone, be sure to send a thank you note reiterating the points you made during the conversation. You will appear more professional and increase your impact. However, don't mail your resume once an interview has been arranged unless it is specifically requested. Take it with you to the interview instead.

Preparing For The Interview

Once the interview has been arranged, begin your in-depth research. You have got to arrive at the interview knowing the company upside down and inside out. You need to know their products, their types of customers, their subsidiaries, their parent, their principal locations, their rank in the industry, their sales and profit trends, their type of ownership, their size, their current plans and much more. By this time you have probably narrowed your job search to one industry, but if you haven't then you need to be familiar with the trends in this firm's industry, the firm's principal competitors and their relative performance, and the direction that the industry leaders are headed. Dig into every resource you can! Read the company literature, the trade press, the business press, and if the company is public, call your stockbroker and ask for still additional information. If possible, speak to someone at the firm before the interview, or if not, speak to someone at a competing firm. Clearly the more time you spend, the better. Even if you feel extremely pressed for time, you should set aside at least 12 hours for pre-interview research.

If you have been out of the job market for some time, don't be surprised if you find yourself tense during your first few interviews. It will probably happen every time you re-enter the market, not just when you seek your first job after getting out of school.

Tension is natural during an interview, but if you can be relaxed you will have an advantage over the competition. Knowing you have done a thorough research job should help you relax for an interview. Also make a list of questions that you think might be asked in an interview. Think out your answers carefully. Then practice reviewing them with a friend. Tape record your responses to the questions he/she raises in the role as interviewer. If you feel particularly unsure of your interviewing skills, arrange your first interviews at firms in which you are not very interested. (But remember it is common courtesy to seem excited about the possibility of working for any firm at which you interview.) Then practice again on your own after these first few interviews. Go over each of the questions that you were asked.

How important is the proper dress for a job interview? Buying a complete wardrobe of Brooks Brothers pinstripes, donning new wing tip shoes and having your hair trimmed every morning is not enough to guarantee your obtaining a career position as an investment banker. But on the other hand, if you can't find a clean, conservative suit and a narrow tie, or won't take the time to polish your shoes and trim and wash your hair—then you are just wasting your time by interviewing at all.

Very rarely will the final selection of candidates for a job opening be determined by dress. So don't spend a fortune on a new wardrobe. But be sure that your clothes are adequate. Men applying for any professional position should wear a suit; women should either wear a dress or a suit (not a pant suit.) Your clothes should be at least as formal or slightly more formal and more conservative than the position would suggest.

Top personal grooming is more important than finding the perfect clothes for a job interview. Careful grooming indicates both a sense of thoroughness and self-confidence.

Be sure that your clothes fit well and that they are immaculate. Hair must be neat and clean. Shoes should be newly polished. Women need to avoid excessive jewelry and excessive makeup. Men should be freshly shaven, even if the interview is late in the day.

Be complete. Everyone needs a watch and a pen and pad of paper (for taking notes.) Finally a briefcase or folder (containing extra copies of your resume) will help complete the look of professionalism.

Sometimes the interviewer will be running behind schedule. Don't be upset, be sympathetic. He/she might be under pressure to interview a lot of candidates and to quickly fill a demanding position. So be sure to come to your interview with good reading material to keep yourself occupied. This will help increase your patience and ease your tenseness.

The Interview

The very beginning of the interview is the most important part because it determines the rapport for the rest of it. Those first few moments are especially crucial. Do you smile when you meet? Do you establish enough eye contact, but not too much? Do you walk into the office with a self-assured and confident stride? Do you shake hands firmly? Do you make small talk easily without being garrulous? It is human nature to judge people by that first impression, so make sure it is a good one. But most of all, try to be yourself.

Often the interviewer will begin, after the small talk, by proceeding to tell you about the company, the division, the department, or perhaps, the position. Because of your detailed research, the information about the company will be repetitive for you and the interviewer would probably like nothing better than to avoid this regurgitation of the company biography. So if you can do so tactfully, indicate to the interviewer that you are very familiar with the firm. If he/she seems intent on providing you with background information, despite your hints, then acquiesce. But be sure to remain attentive. If you can manage to generate a brief discussion of the company or the industry at this point, without being forceful, great. It will help to further build rapport, underscore your interests and increase your impact.

Soon (if it didn't begin that way) the interviewer will begin the questions. This period of the interview falls into one of two categories (or somewhere in between): either a structured interview, where the interviewer has a prescribed set of questions to ask; or an unstructured interview, where the in-

---

Some Favorite Interview Questions

Tell me about yourself...

Why did you leave your last job?

What excites you in your current job?

What are your career goals?

Where would you like to be in 5 years?

What are your greatest strengths?

What are your greatest weaknesses?

Why do you wish to work for this firm?

Where else are you seeking employment?

Why should we hire you? ■

terviewer will ask only leading questions to get you to talk about yourself, your experiences and your goals. Try to sense as quickly as possible which direction the interviewer wishes to proceed and follow along in the direction he/she seems to be leading. This will make the interviewer feel more relaxed and in control of the situation.

Many of the questions will be similar to the ones that you were expecting and you will have prepared answers. Remember to keep attuned to the interviewer and make the length of your answers appropriate to the situation. If you are really unsure as to how detailed a response the interviewer is seeking, then ask. Query if he/she would prefer more details of a particular aspect.

As the interview progresses, the interviewer will probably mention what he/she considers to be the most important responsibilities of the position. If applicable, draw parallels between your experience and the demands of the position as seen by the interviewer. Describe your past experience in the same manner that you did on your resume: emphasizing results and achievements and not merely describing activities. If you listen carefully (listening is a very important part of the interviewing process) the interviewer might very well mention or imply the skills in terms of what he/she is seeking. But don't exaggerate. Be on the level.

Try not to cover too much ground during the first interview. This interview is often the toughest, with many candidates being screened out. If you are interviewing for a very competitive position, you will have to make an impression that will last. Focus on a few of your greatest strengths that are relevant to the position. Develop these points carefully, state them again in other words, and then try to summarize them briefly at the end of the interview.

Often the interviewer will pause towards the end and ask if you have any questions. Particularly in a structured interview, this might be the one chance to really show your knowledge of and interest in the firm. Have prepared a list of specific questions that are of real interest to you. Let your questions subtly show your research and your knowledge of the firm's activities. It is wise to have an extensive list of questions, as several of them may have already been answered during the interview.

Do not allow your opportunity to ask questions to become an interrogation. Avoid bringing your list of questions to the interview. And ask questions that you are fairly certain the interviewer can answer (remember how you feel when you cannot answer a question during an interview.)

Even if you are unable to determine the salary range beforehand, do not ask about it during the first interview. You can always ask about it later. Above all, don't ask about fringe benefits until you have been offered a position. (Then be sure to get all the details.) You should be able to determine the company's policy on fringe benefits relatively easily before the interview.

Try not to be negative about anything during the interview. (Particularly any past employer or any previous job.) Be cheerful. Everyone likes to work with someone who seems to be happy.

Don't let a tough question throw you off base. If you don't know the answer to a question, say so simply — do not apologize. Just smile. Nobody can answer every question — particularly some of the questions that are asked in job interviews.

Before your first interview, you may have been able to determine how many interviews the employer usually has for positions at your level. (Of course it may differ quite a bit within one firm.) Usually you can count on at least three or four interviews, although some firms, such as some of the professional partnerships, are well-known to give a minimum of six interviews for all professional positions.

Depending on what information you are able to obtain you might want to vary your strategy quite a bit from interview to interview. For instance if the first interview is a

You're Fired!!

You are not the first and will not be the last to go through this traumatic experience. Thousands of professionals are fired every week. Remember, being fired is not a reflection on you as a person. It is usually a reflection of your company's staffing needs and its perception of your recent job performance. Share the fact with your relatives and friends. Being fired is not something of which to be ashamed.

Don't start your job search with a flurry of unplanned activity. Start by choosing a strategy and working out a plan. Now is not the time for major changes in your life. If possible, remain in the same career and in the same geographical location, at least until you have been working again for a while. On the other hand, if the only industry for which you are trained is leaving, or is severely depressed in your area, then you should give prompt consideration to moving or switching careers.

Register for unemployment compensation immediately. A thorough job search could take months. After all, your employers have been contributing to unemployment insurance specifically for you ever since your first job. Don't be surprised to find other professionals collecting unemployment compensation as well. Unemployment compensation is for everybody who is between jobs.

Be prepared for the question, "Why were you fired?", during job interviews. Avoid mentioning you were fired while arranging interviews. Try especially hard not to speak negatively of your past employer and not to sound particularly worried about your status of being temporarily unemployed. But don't spend much time reflecting on why you were fired or how you might have avoided it. Look ahead. Think positively. And be sure to follow a careful plan during your job search. ■

screening interview then try to have a few of your strengths really stand out. On the other hand, if later interviews are primarily with people who are in a position to veto your hiring, but not to push it forward (and few people are weeded out at these stages), then you should primarily focus on building rapport as opposed to reiterating and developing your key strengths.

If it looks as though your skills and background do not match the position your interviewer was hoping to fill, ask him or her if there is another division or subsidiary that perhaps could profit from your talents.

After The Interview

Write a follow-up letter immediately after the interview, while it is still fresh in the interviewer's mind. Then, if you have not heard from the interviewer within seven days, call him/her to stress your continued interest in the firm and the position and to request a second interview.

A parting word of advice. Again and again during your job search you will be rejected. You will be rejected when you apply for interviews. You will be rejected after interviews. For every job you finally receive you will probably have received a multitude of rejections. Don't let these rejections slow you down. Keep reminding yourself that the sooner you go out and get started on your job search and get those rejections flowing in, the closer you will be to obtaining the better job.

RESUMES AND COVER LETTERS

1. Resume Preparation
2. Resume Format
3. Resume Content
4. Should You Hire A Resume Writer?
5. Cover Letters

6. Sample Resumes
7. General Model For A Cover Letter
8. Sample Cover Letters
9. General Model For A Follow-up Letter

Resumes/Overview

When filling a position, a recruiter will often have 100 plus applicants, but time to interview only the 5 or 10 most promising ones. So he or she will have to reject most applicants after a brief skimming of their resume.

Unless you have phoned and talked to the recruiter—which you should do whenever you can—you will be chosen or rejected for an interview entirely on the basis of your resume and cover letter. So your resume must be outstanding. (But remember—a resume is no substitute for a job search campaign. YOU must seek a job. Your resume is only one tool.)

Resume Preparation

One page, usually.
Unless you have an unusually strong background with many years of experience and a large diversity of outstanding achievements, prepare a one page resume. Recruiters dislike long resumes.

8½ x 11 Size
Recruiters often get resumes in batches of hundreds. If your resume is on small sized paper it is likely to get lost in the pile. If oversized, it is likely to get crumpled at the edges, and won't fit in their files.

Typesetting

Modern photocomposition typesetting gives you the clearest, sharpest image, a wide variety of type styles and effects such as italics, bold facing, and book-like justified margins. Typesetting is the best resume preparation process, but is also the most expensive.

Word Processing

The most flexible way to get your resume typed is on a good quality word processor. With word processing, you can make changes almost instantly because your resume will be stored on a magnetic disk and the computer will do all the re-typing automatically. A word processing service will usually offer you a variety of type styles in both regular and proportional spacing. You can have bold facing for emphasis, justified margins, and clear, sharp copies.

Typing

Household typewriters and office typewriters with nylon or other cloth ribbons are NOT good for typing the resume you will have printed. If you can't get word processing or typesetting, hire a professional with a high quality office typewriter with a plastic ribbon (usually called a "carbon ribbon.")

Printing

Find the best quality offset printing process available. DO NOT make your copies on an office photocopier. Only the personnel office may see the resume you mail. Everyone else may see only a copy of it. Copies of copies quickly become unreadable. Some professionally maintained, extra-high-quality photocopiers are of adequate quality, if you are in a rush. But top quality offset printing is best.

Proofread your resume

Whether you typed it yourself or had it written, typed, or typeset, mistakes on resumes can be embarrassing, particularly when something obvious such as your name is misspelled. No matter how much you paid someone else to type or write or typeset your resume, YOU lose if there is a mistake. So proofread it as carefully as possible. Get a friend to help you. Read your draft aloud as your friend checks the proof copy. Then have your friend read aloud while you check. Next, read it letter by letter to check spelling and punctuation.

If you are having it typed or typeset by a resume service or a printer, and you can't bring a friend or take the time during the day to proof it, pay for it and take it home. Proof it there and bring it back later to get it corrected and printed.

Resume Format

Basic data
Your name, phone number, and a complete address should be at the top of your resume. (If you are a university student, you should also show your home address and phone number.)

Separate your education and work experience
In general, list your experience first. If you have recently graduated, list your education first, unless your experience is more important than your education. (For example, if you have just graduated from a teaching school, have some business experience and are applying for a job in business you would list your business experience first.) If you have two or more years of college, you don't need to list high schools.

Reverse chronological order
To a recruiter your last job and your latest schooling are the most important. So put the last first and list the rest going back in time.

Show dates and locations

Put the dates of your employment and education on the left of the page. Put the names of the companies you worked for and the schools you attended a few spaces to the right of the dates. Put the city and state or city and country where you studied or worked to the right of the page.

Avoid sentences and large blocks of type

Your resume will be scanned, not read. Short, concise phrases are much more effective than long-winded sentences. Keep everything easy to find. Avoid paragraphs longer than six lines. Never go ten or more lines in a paragraph. If you have more than six lines of information about one job or school, put it in two or more paragraphs.

Resume Content

Be factual

In many companies, inaccurate information on a resume or other application material will get you fired as soon as the inaccuracy is discovered. Protect yourself.

Be positive

You are selling your skills and accomplishments in your resume. If you achieved something, say so. Put it in the best possible light. Don't hold back or be modest, no one else will. But don't exaggerate to the point of misrepresentation.

Be brief

Write down the important (and pertinent) things you have done, but do it in as few words as possible. The shorter your resume is, the more carefully it will be examined.

Work experience
Emphasize continued experience in a particular type of function or continued interest in a particular industry. De-emphasize irrelevant positions. Delete positions that you held for less than four months. (Unless you are a very recent college grad or still in school.)

Stress your results
Elaborate on how you contributed to your past employers. Did you increase sales, reduce costs, improve a product, implement a new program? Were you promoted?

Mention relevant skills and responsibilities
Be specific. Slant your past accomplishments toward the type of position that you hope to obtain. Example: Do you hope to supervise people? Then state how many people, performing what function, you have supervised.

Education
Keep it brief if you have more than two years of career experience. Elaborate more if you have less experience. Mention degrees received and any honors or special awards. Note individual courses or research projects that might be relevant for employers. For instance, if you are a liberal arts major, be sure to mention courses in such areas as: accounting, statistics, computer programming, or mathematics.

Job objective?
Leave it out. Even if you are certain of exactly the type of job that you desire, the inclusion of a job objective might eliminate you from consideration for other positions that a recruiter feels are a better match for your qualifications.

Personal data
Keep it very brief. Two lines maximum. A one-word mention of commonly practiced activities such as golf, skiing, sailing,

chess, bridge, tennis, etc. can prove to be good way to open up a conversation during an interview. Do not include your age, weight, height, etc.

Should You Hire A Resume Writer?

If you write reasonably well, there are some advantages to writing your resume yourself. To write it well, you will have to review your experience and figure out how to explain your accomplishments in clear, brief phrases. This will help you when you explain your work to interviewers.

If your write your resume, everything in it will be in your own words—it will sound like you. It will say what you want it to say. And you will be much more familiar with the contents. If you are a good writer, know yourself well and have a good idea of what parts of your background employers are looking for, you may be able to write your own resume better than anyone else can. If you write your resume yourself, you should have someone who can be objective (preferably not a close relative) review it with you.

When should you have your resume professionally written? If you have difficulty writing in Resume Style (which is quite unlike normal written language), if you are unsure of which parts of your background you should emphasize, or if you think your resume would make your case better if it did not follow the standard form outlined here or in a book on resumes, then you should have it professionally written.

There are two reasons even some professional resume writers we know have had their resumes written with the help of fellow professionals. First, when they need the help of someone who can be objective about their background, and second, when they want an experienced sounding board to help focus their thoughts.

If you decide to hire a resume writer
The best way to choose a writer is by reputation—the recommendation of a friend, a personnel director, your school placement officer or someone else knowledgeable in the field.

You should ask, "If I'm not satisfied with what you write, will you go over it with me and change it?"

You should ask, "How long has the person who will write my resume been writing resumes?"

There is no sure relation between price and quality, except that you are unlikely to get a good writer for less than $50 for an uncomplicated resume and you shouldn't have to pay more than $300 unless your experience is very extensive or complicated. There will be additional charges for printing.

Few resume services will give you a firm price over the phone, simply because some people's resumes are too complicated and take too long to do at any predetermined price. Some services will quote you a price that applies to almost all of their customers. Be sure to do some comparative shopping. Obtain a firm price before you engage their services and find out how expensive minor changes will be.

Cover Letters

Always mail a cover letter with your resume. In a cover letter you can show an interest in the company that you can't show in a resume. You can point out one or two skills or accomplishments the company can put to good use.

Make it personal
The more personal you can get, the better. If someone known to the person you are writing has recommended that you contact the company, get permission to include his/her name in the letter. If you have the name of a person to send the letter to, make sure you have the name spelled correctly and address it directly to that person. Be sure to put the person's

name and title on both the letter and envelope. This will ensure that your letter will get through to the proper person, even if a new person now occupies this position. But even if you are addressing it to the "Personnel Director" or the "Hiring Partner," send a letter.

Type cover letters in full. Don't try the cheap and easy ways like photocopying the body of your letter and typing in the inside address and salutation. You will give the impression that you are mailing to a multitude of companies and have no particular interest in any one. Have your letters fully typed and signed with a pen.

Phone
Precede or follow your mailing with a phone call.

Bring extra copies of your resume to the interview
If the person interviewing you doesn't have your resume, be prepared. Carry copies of your own. Even if you have already forwarded your resume, be sure to take extra copies to the interview, as someone other than the interviewer(s) might now have the first copy you sent.

Chronological Resume

JAMES WASHINGTON WHITE, JR.

U.S. Address:
486 East 77th Street
New York, New York 10021
(212) 212-2121

Jamaican Address:
Room 1234
Playboy Jamaica, Ltd.
Doctor's Beach, Jamaica
(809) 326-1312

experience

1984-present | **PLAYBOY, JAMAICA LTD.**   **Doctor's Beach, Jamaica**
Resident Engineer for this publicly owned resort with main offices in Chicago, Illinois. Responsibilities include:
- Maintain electrical generating equipment.
- Supervise an eight-member staff in maintenance of refrigeration equipment, power and light generators, water purification plant, and general construction machinery.

1982-1984 | **NIGRIL BEACH HOTEL**   **Nigril Beach, Jamaica**
Resident Engineer for a privately-held resort, assigned total responsibility for facility generating equipment.
- Directed maintenance, operation and repair of diesel generating equipment.

1980-1982 | Directed overhaul of turbo generating equipment in two Mid-Western localities and assisted in overhaul of a turbo generating unit in Mexico.

1975-1980 | **CAPITAL CITY ELECTRIC**   **Washington, D.C.**
Service Engineer for the power generation service division of this regional power company, supervised the overhaul, maintenance and repair of large generators and associated auxiliary equipment.

other experience | A Night File Supervisor for Columbia Mutual Life Insurance Company (1973-1975) and an Apprentice Welder at the Potomac Naval Shipyard from 1971-1972.

Volunteer Co-ordinator Washington D.C. NAACP 1979; Activities Co-Chairman 1978.

education

1972-1975 | **Franklin Institute**   **Baltimore, Maryland**
Awarded a degree of Associate of Engineering. Concentration in Mechanical Power Engineering Technology.

personal | Willing to travel and relocate.
Interested in sailing, scuba diving, deep sea fishing.

References available upon request.

Functional Resume

MARGARET COPLEY

420 Boylston Street
Pittsburgh, Pennsylvania 15234
412/323-2491

Solid background in plate making, separations, color matching, background definition, printing, mechanicals, color corrections, and supervision of personnel. A highly motivated manager, adept problem-solver and effective communicator. Proven ability to:

- Create Commercial Graphics
- Produce Embossing Drawings
- Color Separate
- Analyze Consumer Acceptance

- Meet Graphic Deadlines
- Control Quality
- Resolve Printing Problems
- Expedite Printing Operations

Qualifications *Printing*—Black and white and color. Can judge acceptability of color reproduction by comparing it with original. Can make four or five color corrections on all media. Have long developed ability to restyle already reproduced four-color artwork. Can create perfect tone for black and white match fill-ins for resume cover letters.

Customer Relations—Work well with customers to assure specifications are met and customers are satisfied. Can guide work through entire production process and strike a balance between technical printing capabilities and need for customer approval.

Management—Schedule work to meet deadlines. Direct staff in production procedures. Control budgets, maintain quality control from inception of project through final approval for printing.

Specialities—Make silk screen overlays for a multitude of processes. Velo bind, GBC bind, perfect bind, gold leaf embossing, silver inlay stamping. Have knowledge to prepare posters, flyers, business cards, and personalized stationery.

Personnel Supervision—Foster an atmosphere that encourages highly talented artists to balance high level creativity with a maximum of production. Have managed a group of over 20 photographers, developers, plate etchers, checkers and artists. Met or beat production deadlines. Am continually instructing new employees, apprentices and students in both artistry and technical operations.

Experience *Assistant Production Manager*, Artsign Digraphics, Erie, PA (1982-Present) Part time.

Professor of Graphic Arts, Pennsylvania College of Fine Arts, Pittsburgh, PA (1980-Present).

Education Massachusetts Conservatory of Art PhD, 1980.

General Model for A Cover Letter

Your
Address

Date

Contact Person Name
Title
Company
Address

Dear Mr. (Ms.) _____:

Immediately explain why your background makes you the best candidate for the position that you are applying for. Keep the first paragraph short and hard-hitting.

Detail what you could contribute to this company. Show how your qualifications will benefit this firm. Remember to keep this letter short; few recruiters will read a cover letter longer than half-a-page.

Describe your interest in the corporation. Subtly emphasize your knowledge about this firm (the result of your research effort) and your familiarity with the industry. It is common courtesy to act extremely eager to work for any company that you interview.

In the closing paragraph you should specifically request an interview. Include your phone number and the hours when you can best be reached. Alternatively, you might prefer to mention that you will follow-up with a phone call (to arrange an interview at a mutually convenient time) within the next several days.

Sincerely yours,

(signature)

Full Name (typed)

Enc. Resume

Cover Letter

49 Smith Park Circle
Houston, Texas 77031

March 15, 1991

Mr. Clinton P. Thomas
Vice President and Director of Personnel
Riverbay Fire Insurance Group
Riverbay Plaza
Houston, Texas 77035

Dear Mr. Thomas:

I am the career oriented individual who can successfully provide technical direction and training to pension analysts in connection with FKLE system.

My major and most recent background is directly involved in the administration of pension and profit sharing plans with TRMZ. Furthermore, my extensive experience both as a Group Pension Pre-Scale Underwriter and as a Pension Underwriter involves data processing knowledge and overall pension administration.

A prime function of mine is decision making with reference to group pension business. You can specifically seek an individual who can recommend changes and/or new procedures of plan administration and maintenance plus assistance in development of pension administration kits for use by the field force at Riverbay. I feel that I possess the ability to fulfill your need dramatically.

I would welcome the practical opportunity to work directly with general agents and plan trustees in qualifying, revising and requalifying pension and profit sharing plans required by TRMZ. You will note in my resume my background in working with others in both an advisory and shirt-sleeve capacity.

I look forward to hearing from you.

Sincerely,

Samuel A. Williams

Enc. Resume

271

General Model For A Follow-up Letter

Your
Address

Date

Contact Person Name
Title
Company
Address

Dear Mr. (Ms.) _____:

Remind the interviewer of the position for which you were interviewed, as well as the date. Thank him (her) for the interview.

Confirm your interest in the opening and the organization. Use specifics to emphasize both that you have researched the firm in detail and considered how you would fit into the company and the position.

Like in your cover letter, emphasize one or two of your strongest qualifications and slant them toward the various points that the interviewer considered the most important for the position. Keep the letter brief, a half-page is plenty.

If appropriate, close with a suggestion for further action, such as a desire to have additional interviews. Mention your phone number and the hours that you can best be reached. Alternatively, you may prefer to mention that you will follow-up with a phone call in several days.

Sincerely yours,

(signature)

Your Full Name (typed)
phone number (if not in text)